Whether you are encountering German speakers in Europe or meeting them here,

whether you are facing a restaurant menu or a hotel desk clerk,

whether you are visiting a museum or stopping at a gas station,

whether you need directions or want to strike up a casual conversation,

whether you have to deal with a medical emergency or a mechanical breakdown,

whether you want to establish trust and good feelings in a business meeting or demonstrate warmth and courtesy in personal dealings, this one book is your—

PASSPORT TO GERMAN

REVISED AND EXPANDED EDITION

REVISED AND EXPANDED EDITION
CHARLES BERLITZ
PASSPORT TO

GERMAN

A SIGNET BOOK

Copyright © 1972 by Charles-François Bertin
Copyright © 1986 by Charles Berlitz

Published by arrangement with Charles Berlitz

SIGNET, SIGNET CLASSIC, MENTOR, ONYX, PLUME, MERIDIAN
and NAL BOOKS are published by New American Library, a division of
Penguin Books USA Inc., 1633 Broadway, New York, New York 10019

First Signet Printing, April, 1974
First Printing (Revised and Expanded Edition), May, 1986

3 4 5 6 7 8 9 10

Contents

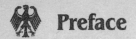# Preface

Is it possible to learn to speak German from a phrase book? If one means basic communication—the ability to speak, understand, and generally get along—the answer is yes, *if* you learn the right phrases. The secret of learning languages is to learn not only individual words but the phrases in which they are apt to occur with frequency, as Germans, Austrians, and Swiss use them every day.

The concept of this book is to provide instant communication in German. The phrases are short, geared to situations of daily life, and pinpointed for easy reference so that you can find the exact section you need at any moment.

There is even a chapter—"Words That Show You Are 'With It' "—which gives you the key words and phrases that German people use to add color to their conversation. In this way, instead of learning about "the umbrella of my aunt," you learn to use the right phrase at the right time, in the very way a German person would use it. And, so that German people will understand your accent, all you have to do is read the phonetic line under each German phrase *as if it were English*. Further practice and listening to German people speak will help you constantly improve your accent.

The use of this book is not limited to a trip to Germany, Austria, or Switzerland. German is an important world language, and besides the pleasure and help you will get by speaking German on your travels, you will enjoy using the idiomatic German phrases in this book in German restaurants or stores at home and with German-speaking people you may meet anywhere.

Travelers using phrase books sometimes complain that when they ask a question or make a request to a native speaker of the language they cannot understand the answer they get. This has been solved in *Passport to German* by an original and effective expedient. After the first few sections a special insert called "Point to the Answer" appears at the end of various sections. You simply show this section, which requests the person to whom you are speaking in German to point to the appropriate answer. This is an assured way of instant and exact communication, and besides its evident usefulness, it will give added confidence. Since you are communicating in this way with a German-speaking person, it also will constantly improve your understanding of the language.

Students studying German in a more conventional manner in school or college will find this book an invaluable aid to their studies in that it brings modern colloquial German alive as a means of communication.

The use of this book will more than double your enjoyment of a trip abroad and also help you save money. Besides the economic factor, why visit a foreign country if you can't break the language barrier and communicate with the new and interesting people you meet? You might as well stay home and see the palaces and monuments of the country on color TV. Who wants to be limited to one language when picking up another language can be so easy and enjoyable?

One can speak and understand current everyday German with comparatively few words and phrases—perhaps 1,600 to 1,900, which is less than the number given in the special dictionary at the end of this book. By using the same short constructions over and over, in the various situations where they normally occur, you will acquire them without conscious effort. They will become a part of your own vocabulary and of your memory bank, and that is, after all, the only secret of learning a language.

How to Acquire an Instant German Accent

Every word or sentence in this book is presented in English, in German, and in an easy-to-read phonetic system that shows you how to pronounce the German correctly. Just pronounce the phonetics as if you were reading English, remembering the following special points:

Syllables printed in capital letters should be stressed.

The syllables are separated by hyphens, except the verb ending **-en,** which is to be pronounced almost as a part of the preceding syllable and for that reason is separated just by an apostrophe. (The apostrophe is also sometimes used between sounds within a syllable to help you see more easily how to pronounce them.)

To pronounce the sound of the special symbol *ů* used in the phonetics, say "ee" but with your lips rounded in a tight little circle as if to whistle. The small circle is to remind you to round your lips.

When you see the combination of letters *kh* in the phonetics, pronounce it with a guttural, throaty sound—like a rough "h" deep in the throat.

When *er* is used in the phonetics and the spelling in the German word is ö, pronounce it as in the English word "fern" but make the "r" as silent as possible. (Of course, when the letter **r** appears in the German spelling, then you should pronounce it fully.)

The letter *g* is always pronounced as in "go" or "get," never as in "gem." To help you remember this, we have spelled it *gh* in the phonetics when it comes before an *e* or an *i.*

The combination *ow* in the phonetics is always pronounced as in "how now, brown cow." We have put an apostrophe before it in such syllables as *l'ow* and *t'ow* to remind you not to pronounce them like the English words "low" and "tow."

The German pronunciation is made clear in the phonetic lines in this book, but it will be helpful for you in reading any other written German you may encounter if you also remember the following differences between German and English spelling and pronunciation:

b when it comes at the end of a word is pronounced *p*.

d when it comes at the end of a word is pronounced *t*.

g when it comes at the end of a word is pronounced *k* (or with the guttural *kh* sound in the combination **-ig**).

j is pronounced like the English *y*.

qu is pronounced *kv*.

v is pronounced like English *f*.

w is pronounced like English *v*.

s when it comes at the beginning of a word and usually in the middle of a word is pronounced like English *z*. At the end of a word it is always pronounced *ss*.

sp and **st** at the beginning of a word are pronounced *shp* and *sht* respectively.

The special German letter **ß** (called *"ess-ts'et"*) is pronounced *ss*.

z is pronounced *ts*.

ch is the guttural *kh* sound.

sch is pronounced like English *sh*.

The vowels **a, e, i, o,** and **u** are pronounced *ah, eh, ee* (or *ih*), *oh,* and *oo* respectively.

ei is pronounced like the English word "eye," and **ie** is pronounced *ee;* **eu** is pronounced *oy*.

When the vowels are written in German with two dots over them, they are called "umlauts," and their approximate pronunciations are as follows: **ä,** *eh;* **äu,** *oy;* **ö,** like *er* but with the sound of the "r" silent, and **ü,** like *ee* with the lips tightly rounded.

If you follow the advice we have given you and the simple phonetics under each word in the book, you are certain to be told:

Sie haben eine sehr gute Aussprache!
zee HAHB'en INE-eh zair GOOT-eh OWSS-shpra-kheh!

which means, "You have a very good accent!"

1. Greetings and Introductions

Mr.	**Mrs.**	**Miss**
Herr	Frau	Fräulein
hair	*frow*	*FROY-line*

Good morning!	**Good day.**	**Good evening.**
Guten Morgen!	Guten Tag.	Guten Abend.
GOO-ten MOR-ghen!	*GOO-ten tahk.*	*GOO-ten AH-bent.*

How are you?	**Fine, thanks, and you?**
Wie geht es Ihnen?	Gut, danke, und Ihnen?
vee gait ess EEN-en?	*goot, DAHN-keh, oont EEN-en?*

Come in, please.	**Sit down, please!**
Kommen Sie herein, bitte.	Nehmen Sie Platz, bitte!
KOHM'en zee hair-INE, BIT-teh.	*NAIM'en zee plahts, BIT-teh!*

My name is Krüger.	**What is your name?**
Mein Name ist Krüger.	Wie ist Ihr Name?
mine NA-meh isst KRÜ-gher.	*vee isst eer NA-meh?*

May I introduce _____ .	**Delighted (to meet you).**
Darf ich vorstellen _____ .	Sehr angenehm.
darf ikh FOR-shtel'en _____ .	*zair AHN-gheh-naim.*

Good-bye.	**So long.**	**Good night.**
Auf Wiedersehen.	Bis bald.	Gute Nacht.
owf VEE-der-zain.	*biss bahlt.*	*GOOT-eh nakht.*

1. Pronounce ů like "ee" with your lips in a tight circle.
2. *kh* is a guttural sound.
3. Stress the syllables in capital letters.

In southern Germany, Austria, and Switzerland a general greeting for all occasions is **Grüss' Gott**—the equivalent of "God bless you."

Herr and **Frau** mean "Mr." and "Mrs." when used with a person's last name. **Herr** also means "man" and **Frau** "woman" or "wife." **Fräulein** (Miss) means *young woman* and may be used with or without a last name.

In Southern Germany and Austria the title **Gnädige Frau** *(GNAY-dig-eh frow)* is often used in direct address to a married lady *without* using her last name. But if you know her name, then use simply **Frau** before the name.

2. Basic Expressions

Learn these by heart. You will use them every time you speak German to someone. If you memorize these expressions and the numbers in the next section, you will find that you can ask prices or directions and generally make your wishes known.

Yes.	**No.**	**Perhaps.**
Ja.	Nein.	Vielleicht.
ya.	*nine.*	*feel-LY'KHT.*

Of course.	**Yes indeed.**	**Please.**
Natürlich.	Jawohl.	Bitte.
na-TÜR-likh.	*ya-VOHL.*	*BIT-teh.*

Thank you.	**You are welcome.**
Danke schön.	Bitte sehr.
DAHN-keh shern.	*BIT-teh zair.*

Excuse me.	**I'm sorry.**	**It's all right.**
Entschuldigung.	Es tut mir leid.	Es macht nichts.
ent-SHOOL-dee-goong.	*ess toot meer lite.*	*ess makht nikhts.*

Here.	**There.**	**This.**	**That.**
Hier.	Dort.	Dies.	Das.
heer.	*dort.*	*deess.*	*dahss.*

Do you speak English?	**I speak a little German.**
Sprechen Sie Englisch?	Ich spreche ein wenig Deutsch.
SHPREKH'en zee EHNG-lish?	*ikh SHPREKH-eh ine VAY-nikh doytch.*

---

1. Pronounce *ü* like "ee" with your lips in a tight circle.
2. *kh* is a guttural sound.
3. Stress the syllables in capital letters.

Do you understand?
Verstehen Sie?
fair-SHTAY'en zee?

I understand.
Ich verstehe.
ikh fair-SHTAY-eh.

. . . very well.
. . . sehr gut.
. . . zair goot.

I don't understand.
Ich verstehe nicht.
ikh fair-SHTAY-eh nikht.

Speak slowly, please.
Sprechen Sie langsam, bitte.
*SHPREKH'en zee
   LAHNG-zahm, BIT-teh.*

Repeat, please.
Wiederholen Sie, bitte.
*vee-der-HO-len zee, BIT-
   teh.*

Write it down.
Schreiben Sie es auf.
SHRY-ben zee ess owf.

Who is it?
Wer ist es?
vair isst ess?

Come in!
Herein!
hair-INE!

Don't come in!
Kommen Sie nicht herein!
KOHM'en zee nikht hair-INE!

One moment, please.
Einen Moment, bitte.
INE-en mo-MENT, BIT-teh.

Wait.
Warten Sie.
VAR-ten zee.

Let's go!
Gehen wir!
GAY'en veer!

That's all.
Das ist alles.
dahss isst AHL-less.

What is this?
Was ist das?
vahss isst dahss?

Where is the telephone?
Wo ist das Telefon?
vo isst dahss teh-leh-FOHN?

Where is the rest room?
Wo ist die Toilette?
vo isst dee twa-LET-teh?

For ladies.
Für Damen.
für DA-men.

For men.
Für Herren.
für HAIR-ren.

Show me.
Zeigen Sie mir.
TS'EYE-ghen zee meer.

How much?	It's too much.	Who?
Wieviel?	Das ist zu viel.	Wer?
vee-FEEL?	*dahss isst ts'oo feel.*	*vair?*

I	you	he	she
Ich	Sie	er	sie
ikh	*zee*	*air*	*zee*

it	we	they
es	wir	sie
ess	*veer*	*zee*

How far is it?	How long?
Wie weit ist es?	Wie lange?
vee vite isst ess?	*vee LAHNG-eh?*

How?	Like this.	Not like this.
Wie?	So.	Nicht so.
vee?	*zo.*	*nikht zo.*

It is possible.	It is not possible.
Es ist möglich.	Es ist nicht möglich.
ess isst MERG-likh.	*ess isst nikht MERG-likh.*

When?	Now.	Not now.
Wann?	Jetzt.	Nicht jetzt.
vahn?	*yetst.*	*nikht yetst.*

Later.	That is very good.
Später.	Das ist sehr gut.
SHPAY-ter.	*dahss isst zair goot.*

That is bad.	Really?
Das ist schlecht.	Wirklich?
dahss isst shlekht.	*VEERK-likh?*

---

1. Pronounce *ů* like "ee" with your lips in a tight circle.
2. *kh* is a guttural sound.
3. Stress the syllables in capital letters.

It doesn't matter.	**It's very important.**
Es macht nichts.	Est ist sehr wichtig.
ess mahkht nikhts.	*ess isst zehr VIKH-tikh.*

You should always use **bitte,** which means "please" (and also "You are welcome"), when you ask questions or make requests. It can also function for "Bring me . . . ," "I want . . . ," or "I would like . . . ," etc. Simply say **bitte** followed by the word for whatever you want, which you can find in the dictionary section.

Nicht wahr? as a question can be used to request agreement to something or to mean "Isn't it?" "Isn't that right?" or "Don't you think so?"

When you ask directions or start a conversation with someone you do not know begin by saying **Entschuldigen Zie, bitte.**—"Excuse me, please"—without adding "Sir" or "Madam" as you might in English.

3. Numbers

The numbers are important not only for asking prices (and perhaps to bargain) but for phone numbers, addresses, and telling time. Learn the first twenty by heart and then from 20 to 100 by tens, and you can deal with money **(Geld)**, a telephone number **(eine Telefonnummer),** or an address **(eine Adresse).**

1	2	3	4
eins	zwei	drei	vier
ine'ss	*ts'vy*	*dry*	*feer*

5	6	7	8
fünf	sechs	sieben	acht
fůnf	*zeks*	*ZEE-ben*	*ahkht*

9	10	11	12
neun	zehn	elf	zwölf
noyn	*ts'ayn*	*elf*	*ts'verlf*

13	14	15
dreizehn	vierzehn	fünfzehn
DRY-ts'ayn	*FEER-ts'ayn*	*FŮNF-ts'ayn*

16	17	18
sechzehn	siebzehn	achtzehn
ZEKH-ts'ayn	*ZEEP-ts'ayn*	*AHKH-ts'ayn*

19	20	21
neunzehn	zwanzig	einundzwanzig
NOYN-ts'ayn	*TS'VAHN-ts'ikh*	*INE-oont-ts'vahn-ts'ikh*

---

1. Pronounce *ů* like "ee" with your lips in a tight circle.
2. *kh* is a guttural sound.
3. Stress the syllables in capital letters.

22
zweiundzwanzig
TS'VY-oont-ts'vahn-ts'ikh

23
dreiundzwanzig
DRY-oont-ts'vahn-ts'ikh

24
vierundzwanzig
FEER-oont-ts'vahn-ts-ikh

25
fünfundzwanzig
FÛNF-oont-ts'vahn-ts'ikh

30
dreißig
DRY-sikh

40
vierzig
FEER-ts'ikh

50
fünfzig
FÛNF-ts'ikh

60
sechzig
ZEKH-ts'ikh

70
siebzig
ZEEP-ts'ikh

80
achtzig
AHKH-ts'ikh

90
neunzig
NOYN-ts'ikh

100
(ein) hundert
(ine) HOON-dert

200
zweihundert
TS'VY-hoon-dert

300
dreihundert
DRY-hoon-dert

400
vierhundert
FEER-hoon-dert

500
fünfhundert
FÛNF-hoon-dert

600
sechshundert
ZEKS-hoon-dert

700
siebenhundert
ZEE-ben-hoon-dert

800
achthundert
AHKHT-hoon-dert

900
neunhundert
NOYN-hoondert

1000
eintausend
ine-T'OW-zent

2000
zweitausend
TS'VY-t'ow-zent

3000
dreitausend
DRY-t'ow-zent

100,000
hunderttausend
HOON-dert-t'ow-zent

1,000,000
eine Million
INE-eh MIL-yohn

the first
der erste
dair AIR-steh

the second
der zweite
dair TS'VY-teh

the third
der dritte
dair DRIT-eh

the last	half	zero
der letzte	halb	null
dair LETS-teh	*hahlp*	*nool*

How much? (or) How many?	What number?
Wieviel?	Welche Nummer?
vee-FEEL?	*VEL-kheh NOOM-er?*

The number 2, **zwei,** is often called **zwo** *(ts'vo)* because, especially over the telephone, **zwei** sounds like **drei.**

"The" is **der** for a masculine noun, **die** for a feminine noun, **das** for a neuter noun, all in the singular. For the plural, "the" becomes **die** for all three genders.

---

1. Pronounce ů like "ee" with your lips in a tight circle.
2. *kh* is a guttural sound.
3. Stress the syllables in capital letters.

4. Arrival

Besides talking with airport officials, one of the most important things you will want to do on arrival in Germany, Austria, or Switzerland is to find your way around. In this section you will find some basic "asking your way" questions and answers. We call your attention to the "Point to the Answer" sections, which people can use to *point out* answers to make it easier for you to understand.

Your passport, please.
Ihren Pass, bitte.
EER-en pahss, BIT-teh.

I am here on a visit.
Ich bin hier auf Besuch.
ikh bin heer owf beh-ZOOKH.

For three weeks.
Für drei Wochen.
für dry VO-khen.

I am on a business trip.
Ich bin auf Geschäftsreise.
ikh bin owf ghe-SHEHFTS-rye-zeh.

Where is the baggage?
Wo ist das Gepäck?
vo isst dahss gheh-PECK?

From Flight 40.
Von Flucht vierzig.
vohn flookht FEER-ts'ikh.

This is my baggage.
Das ist mein Gepäck.
dahss isst mine gheh-PECK.

Where is the customs office?
Wo ist das Zollamt?
vo isst dahss TS'OHL-ahmt?

That belongs to me.
Das gehört mir.
dahss gheh-HERT meer.

Shall I open it?
Soll ich es aufmachen?
zoll ikh ess OWF-mahkh'en?

Open it.
Machen Sie es auf.
MAHKH'en zee ess owf.

One moment, please.
Einen Moment, bitte.
INE-en mo-MENT, BIT-teh.

---

1. Pronounce *ü* like "ee" with your lips in a tight circle.
2. *kh* is a guttural sound.
3. Stress the syllables in capital letters.

11

I have nothing to declare.
Ich habe nichts zu verzollen.
ikh HAHB-eh nikhts ts'oo fair-TS'OLL'en.

One moment! A suitcase is missing!
Moment! Es fehlt ein Handkoffer!
mo-MENT! ess faylt ine HAHNT-kof-fer!

Where should I report it?
Wo soll ich das anmelden?
vo zoll ikh dahss AHN-meld-en?

Does this belong to you?
Gehört das Ihnen?
gheh-HERT dahss EE-nen?

Yes indeed!
Jawohl!
ya-VOHL!

Many thanks!
Vielen Dank!
*FEEL'en
dahnk!*

Where is the bus to the city?
Wo ist der Bus zur Stadt?
vo isst dair booss ts'oor shtaht?

Where can I make a phone call?
Wo kann ich telefonieren?
vo kahn ikh teh-leh-foh-NEER'en?

Where is the restaurant?
Wo ist das Restaurant?
vo isst dahss rest-oh-RAHNG?

Where are the rest rooms?
Wo sind die Toiletten?
vo zint dee twah-LET-en?

Porter!
Gepäckträger!
gheh-PAYK-tray-gher!

Take these bags to a taxi.
Bringen Sie diese Koffer zu
   einem Taxi.
*BRING'en zee DEE-zeh
   KOFF-er ts'oo INE-em
   TAHK-see.*

I'll carry this one myself.
Ich trage diesen selbst.
ikh TRAHG-eh DEE-zen zelpst.

How much is it?
Wieviel macht es?
vee-FEEL mahkt ess?

To the Hotel Frankfurter Hof.
Zum Hotel Frankfurter Hof.
ts'oom ho-TEL FRAHNK-foor-ter hohf.

To the Hotel Vier Jahreszeiten, please.
Zum Hotel Vier Jahreszeiten, bitte.
ts'oom ho-TEL feer YAHR-ess-ts'eye-ten, BIT-teh.

Excuse me, how can I go . . .
Verzeihung, wie komme ich . . .
fair-TS'Y-oong, vee KOHM-eh ikh . . .

. . . to the Hotel Kronprinzen?
. . . zum Hotel Kronprinzen?
. . . ts'oom ho-TEL KROHN-prin-ts'en?

. . . to a good restaurant?
. . . zu einem guten Restaurant?
. . . ts'oo INE-em GOOT-en rest-oh-RAHNG?

. . . to this address?
. . . zu dieser Adresse?
. . . ts'oo DEE-zer ah-DRES-seh?

. . . to the movies?
. . . zum Kino?
. . . ts'oom KEE-no?

---

1. Pronounce *ü* like "ee" with your lips in a tight circle.
2. *kh* is a guttural sound.
3. Stress the syllables in capital letters.

. . . to the post office?	**. . . to a police station?**
. . . zur Post?	. . . zur Polizeistation?
. . . ts'oor post?	*. . . ts'oor po-lee-T'SY-shta-ts'yohn?*

. . . to a pharmacy?
. . . zur Apotheke?
. . . ts'oor ah-po-TAYK-eh?

. . . to a hospital?
. . . zu einem Krankenhaus?
. . . ts'oo INE-em KRAHN-ken-howss?

. . . to a barber? (or hairdresser)
. . . zu einem Friseur?
. . . ts'oo INE-em free-ZERR?

. . . to a department store?
. . . zu einem Kaufhaus?
. . . ts'oo INE-em KOWF-howss?

. . . to the American consulate?
. . . zum amerikanischen Konsulat?
. . . ts'oom ah-meh-ree-KAHN-ee-shen kohn-soo-LAHT?

. . . Canadian . . .	**. . . British . . .**
. . . kanadischen . . .	. . . britischen . . .
. . . kah-NA-dee-shen . . .	*. . . BRIT-ee-shen . . .*

Thank you very much.	**Very kind of you.**
Danke vielmals.	Sehr nett von Ihnen.
DAHNK-eh FEEL-mahlss.	*zair net fohn EEN-en.*

POINT TO THE ANSWER

To make sure that you understand the answer to your question show the following section to a German person so he or she can select the answer. The sentence in German after the arrow asks him or her to point to the answer. Other "Point to the Answer" sections appear on pages 22, 36, 42, 44, 47, 55, 59, 71, 103, 226.

 Zeigen Sie bitte hierunter Ihr Antwort auf meine Frage. Vielen Dank.

Es ist in dieser Richtung.
It's that way.

An der _____ Chausée.
On _____ Avenue.

An der _____ Straße.
On _____ Street.

Gerade aus.
Straight ahead.

Rechts.
To the right.

Links.
To the left.

Es ist in der Nähe.
It's near.

Man kann dort spazieren.
You can walk there.

Es ist weit.
It's far.

Nehmen Sie ein taxi.
Take a taxi.

Nehmen Sie den Bus.
Take the bus.

An der Ecke.
On the corner.

Steigen Sie aus an _____ .
Get off at _____ .

Nehmen Sie die U-Bahn.
Take the subway.

---

1. Pronounce *ŭ* like "ee" with your lips in a tight circle.
2. *kh* is a guttural sound.
3. Stress the syllables in capital letters.

5. Hotel—Laundry—Dry Cleaning

Although the staffs of the larger hotels have some training in English, you will find that the use of German makes for better understanding and better relations, especially with the service personnel. We have included laundry and dry cleaning in this section as this is one of the things for which you have to make yourself understood in speaking to the hotel chambermaid or valet.

Can you recommend a good hotel?
Können Sie mir ein gutes Hotel empfehlen?
KERN'en zee meer ine GOOT-es ho-TEL emp-FAIL'en?

. . . a guest house?
. . . einen Gasthof?
. . . INE-en GAHST-hohf?

In the center of town?
Im Zentrum der Stadt?
im TS'EN-troom dair shtaht?

Not too expensive.
Nicht zu teuer.
nikht ts'oo TOY-er.

My name is _____ .
Mein Name ist _____ .
mine NA-meh isst _____ .

I've made a reservation.
Ich habe reservieren lassen.
ikh HAHB-eh reh-zer-VEER'en LAHSS'en.

Have you a room?
Haben Sie ein Zimmer?
HAHB'en zee ine TS'IM-er?

I would like . . .
Ich hätte gern . . .
ikh HET-teh gairn . . .

. . . a single room.
. . . ein Einzelzimmer.
. . . ine INE-ts'el-ts'im-er.

. . . a double room.
. . . ein Doppelzimmer.
. . . ine DOPP-el-ts'im-er.

. . . with two beds.
. . . mit zwei Betten.
. . . mit ts'vy BET-ten.

---

1. Pronounce *ů* like "ee" with your lips in a tight circle.
2. *kh* is a guttural sound.
3. Stress the syllables in capital letters.

. . . **with a bath.**
. . . mit Bad.
. . . *mit baht.*

. . . **with hot water.**
. . . mit heißem Wasser.
. . . *mit HI-sem VAHS-ser.*

. . . **with a balcony.**
. . . mit Balkon.
. . . *mit bahl-KOHN.*

. . . **with a radio.**
. . . mit einem Radio.
. . . *mit INE-em RAH-dee-oh.*

. . . **with TV.**
. . . mit Fernsehen.
. . . *mit FAIRN-zay'en.*

How much does it cost?
Wieviel kostet es?
vee-FEEL KO-stet ess?

. . . **per day?**
. . . pro Tag?
. . . *pro TAHK?*

. . . **per week?**
. . . pro Woche?
. . . *pro VO-kheh?*

Are the meals included?
Sind die Mahlzeiten ein-
   begriffen?
zint dee MAHL-ts'y-ten
   INE-beh-griff'en?

Is breakfast included?
Ist das Frühstück einbegriffen?
isst dahss FRÜ-shtŭk INE-beh-griff'en?

I should like to see it.
Ich möchte das Zimmer sehen.
ikh MERKH-teh dahss TS'IM-er ZAY'en.

Where is the bath?
Wo ist das Bad?
voh isst dahss baht?

. . . **the shower?**
. . . das Brausebad?
. . . *dahss BROW-zeh-baht?*

I'd like another room.
Ich möchte ein anderes Zimmer haben.
ikh MERKH-teh ine AHN-der-ess TS'IM-er HAHB'en.

. . . **on a higher floor.**
. . . in einem höheren Stockwerk.
. . . *in INE-em HER-er-en SHTOCK-vehrk.*

. . . better.	. . . larger.	. . . smaller.
. . . besser.	. . . größer.	. . . kleiner.
. . . BES-ser.	. . . GRERS-ser.	. . . KLINE-er.

I'll take this.	**I'll stay for five days.**
Ich nehme dieses.	Ich bleibe fünf Tage.
ikh NAY-meh DEE-zes.	ikh BLY-beh fünf TA-geh.

About one week.
Ungefähr eine Woche.
OON-gheh-fair INE-eh VO-kheh.

At what time do you serve lunch?
Um wieviel Uhr servieren Sie das Mittagessen?
oom VEE-feel oor zer-VEER'en zee dahss MIT-tahk-ess'en?

At what time do you serve dinner?
Um wieviel Uhr servieren Sie das Abendessen?
oom VEE-feel oor zer-VEER'en zee dahss AH-bent-ess'en?

I would like . . .	**. . . mineral water**	**. . . some ice.**
Ich möchte . . .	. . . Seltzerwasser	. . . etwas Eis
ikh MERKH-teh . . .	. . . ZEL-ts'er-vahs-ser	. . . ET-vahss ice.

Breakfast for Room 405.
Frühstück für Zimmer vierhundertfünf.
FRÜ-shtük für TS'IM-er FEER-hoon-dert-fünf.

Coffee, rolls, and butter.
Kaffee, Brötchen, and Butter.
KA-fay, BRERT-khen, oont BOOT-ter.

For a more complete choice of breakfast foods, see page
31.

---

1. Pronounce ů like "ee" with your lips in a tight circle.
2. kh is a guttural sound.
3. Stress the syllables in capital letters.

Will you send these letters for me?
Würden Sie diese Briefe für mich abschicken?
VÛR-den zee DEE-zeh BREE-feh fûr mikh AHP-shik'en?

Will you put stamps on them?
Würden Sie Marken aufkleben?
VÛR-den zee MAR-ken OWF-clay ben?

My key, please.
Meinen Schlüssel, bitte.
MY-nen SHLÛSS-el, BIT-teh.

Send my mail to this address.
Schicken Sie meine Post an diese Adresse.
SHIK'en zee MY-neh post ahn DEE-zeh ah-DRESS-eh.

Have you mail for me?
Haben Sie Post für mich?
HAHB'en zee post fûr mikh?

I want to speak to the manager.
Ich möchte den Direktor sprechen.
ikh MERKH-teh den dee-REK-tor SHPREKH'en.

I need an interpreter.
Ich brauche einen Dolmetscher.
ikh BROW-kheh INE-en DOHL-meh-cher.

Are you the chambermaid?
Sind Sie das Zimmermädchen?
zint zee dahss TS'IM-er-mayt-yen?

I need . . .	**. . . a blanket.**
Ich brauche . . .	. . . eine Decke.
ikh BROW-kheh . . .	*. . . INE-eh DEK-eh.*
. . . a pillow.	**. . . a towel.**
. . . ein Kissen.	. . . ein Handtuch.
. . . ine KIS-sen.	*. . . ine HAHNT-tookh.*

. . . soap.
. . . Seife.
. . . *ZY-feh.*

. . . toilet paper.
. . . Toilettenpapier.
. . . *twa-LET-ten-pa-peer.*

That is to be cleaned.
Das muß gereinigt werden.
dahss mooss ghe-RINE-nikht VAIRD'en.

That is to be pressed.
Das muß gebügelt werden.
dahss mooss gheh-BÜ-ghelt VAIRD'en.

That is to be washed.
Das muß gewaschen werden.
dahss mooss gheh-VA-shen VAIRD'en.

That is to be repaired.
Das muß repariert werden.
dahss mooss reh-pa-REERT VAIRD'en.

For this evening?
Für heute abend?
für HOY-teh AH-bent?

For . . .tomorrow?
Für . . . morgen?
für . . . MOR-ghen?

. . . tomorrow afternoon?
. . . morgen nachmittag?
. . . *MOR-ghen NAKH-mit-tahk?*

. . . tomorrow evening?
. . . morgen abend?
. . . *MOR-ghen AH-bent?*

Be careful with this.
Seien Sie vorsichtig damit.
ZY'en zee FOR-zikh-tikh da-MIT.

When?
Wann?
vahn?

For sure?
Sicher?
ZIKH-er?

---

1. Pronounce *ü* like "ee" with your lips in a tight circle.
2. *kh* is a guttural sound.
3. Stress the syllables in capital letters.

Are my things ready?
Sind meine Sachen fertig?
zint MY-neh ZAHKH-en FAIR-tikh?

My bill, please.
Meine Rechnung, bitte.
MY-neh REKH-noong, BIT-teh.

I'm leaving tomorrow morning.
Ich reise morgen früh ab.
ikh RY-zeh MOR-ghen frü ahp.

Please call me at seven o'clock.
Bitte rufen Sie mich um sieben Uhr an.
BIT-teh ROOF'en zee mikh oom ZEE-ben oor ahn.

It's very important.
Es ist sehr wichtig.
ess isst zair VIKH-tikh.

When is checkout time?
Wann muss ich das Zimmer frei machen?
vahn mooss ikh dahss ts'im-er fry MAHKH'en?

Hotel floors are generally counted starting above the ground floor—**Erdgeschoß** or **Grundstock**—so that the second floor is called the first, the third the second, etc.

In many hotels you don't have to ask for a shoeshine. Just leave your shoes outside the door as you retire. Not a bad idea, **nicht wahr?** (''isn't that true?'')

POINT TO THE ANSWER

To make sure that you understand the answer to your question, show the following section to a German-speaking person so that he or she can select the answer. The sentence in

German after the arrow asks him or her to point to the answer.

 Zeigen Sie bitte hierunter Ihr Antwort auf meine Frage. Vielen Dank.

Heute.   **Heute abend.**   **Morgen.**
Today.   This evening.   Tomorrow.

Früh.   **Spät.**
Early.   Late.

Vor ein,   **zwei,**   **drei,**   **vier,**   **fünf,**   **sechs Uhr.**
Before one,   two,   three,   four,   five,   six o'clock.

Um sieben,   **acht,**   **neun,**   **zehn,**   **elf,**   **zwölf Uhr.**
At seven,   eight,   nine,   ten,   eleven,   twelve o'clock.

Montag   **Dienstag**   **Mittwoch**   **Donnerstag**
Monday   Tuesday   Wednesday   Thursday

Freitag   **Sonnabend**   **Sonntag**
Friday   (Samstag)   Sunday
                 Saturday

---

1. Pronounce *ǔ* like "ee" with your lips in a tight circle.
2. *kh* is a guttural sound.
3. Stress the syllables in capital letters.

6. Time: Hours—Days— Months

In the "Hotel" section you noted that when making an appointment at a certain hour you simply put **um** in front of the number followed by **Uhr** (hour). The following section shows you how to tell time in greater detail, including dates. You can make all sorts of arrangements with people by indicating the hour, the day, the date, and adding **Einverstanden?**—"Is it agreed?" or "Okay?"

What time is it?	**It is one o'clock.**	**It is six o'clock.**
Wie spät ist es?	Es ist ein Uhr.	Es ist sechs Uhr.
vee shpayt isst ess?	*ess isst ine oor.*	*ess ist zex oor.*

six thirty or **half past six**
sechs Uhr dreißig (or) halb sieben
zex oor DRY-sikh   hahlp ZEE-ben

a quarter past seven	**a quarter to eight**
viertel nach sieben	viertel vor acht
FEER-tel nahkh ZEE-ben	*FEER-tel for ahkht*

ten minutes past ten
zehn Minuten nach zehn
ts'ayn mee-NOOT-en nahkh ts'ayn

ten minutes to three	**at nine o'clock**
zehn Minuten vor drei	um neun Uhr
ts'ayn mee-NOOT-en for dry	*oom noyn oor*

exactly nine o'clock	**the morning**
punkt neun Uhr	der Morgen
poonkt noyn oor	*dair MOR-ghen*

---

1. Pronounce *ů* like "ee" with your lips in a tight circle.
2. *kh* is a guttural sound.
3. Stress the syllables in capital letters.

noon
der Mittag
dair MIT-tahk

the afternoon
der Nachmittag
dair NAKH-mit-tahk

the evening
der Abend
dair AH-bent

the night
die Nacht
dee nakht

today
heute
HOY-teh

yesterday
gestern
GUESS-tern

the day before yesterday
vorgestern
FOR-guess-tern

tomorrow
morgen
MOR-ghen

the day after tomorrow
übermorgen
Ü-BER-mor-ghen

this morning
heute Morgen
HOY-teh MOR-ghen

tomorrow morning
morgen früh
MOR-ghen frü

this evening
heute Abend
HOY-teh AH-bent

tomorrow evening
morgen Abend
MOR-ghen AH-bent

last night
gestern Abend
GUESS-tern AH-bent

our last evening here
unser letzter Abend hier
OON-zer LET-ster AH-bent heer

this week
diese Woche
DEE-zeh VO-kheh

last week
vorige Woche
FOR-ig-eh VO-kheh

next week
nächste Woche
NAYK-steh VO-kheh

two weeks ago
vor zwei Wochen
for ts'vy VO-khen

this month
diesen Monat
DEE-zen MO-naht

next month
nächsten Monat
NAYK-sten MO-naht

several months ago
vor einigen Monaten
for INE-ig-en MO-naht-en

this year
dieses Jahr
DEE-zes yar

last year
voriges Jahr
FOR-ig-ess yar

next year
nächstes Jahr
NEK-stehs yar

five years ago
vor fünf Jahren
for fünf YAR-en

1990
neunzehnhundertneunzig
NOYN-ts'ayn-hoon-dert-
   NOYN-ts'ikh

Monday
Montag
MOHN-tahk

Tuesday
Dienstag
DEENSS-tahk

Wednesday
Mittwoch
MIT-vohkh

Thursday
Donnerstag
DOH-nerss-tahk

Friday
Freitag
FRY-tahk

Saturday
Samstag (or) Sonnabend
ZAHMSS-tahk ZOHN-ah-bent

Sunday
Sonntag
ZOHN-tahk

next Monday
nächsten Montag
NAYK-sten MOHN-tahk

every Sunday
jeden Sonntag
YAY-den ZOHN-tahk

last Tuesday
vorigen Dienstag
FOR-ig-en DEENSS-tahk

on Fridays
Freitags
FRY-tahks

January
Januar
YA-noo-ar

February
Februar
FEB-roo-ar

March
März
mairts

April
April
ah-PREEL

May
Mai
my

June
Juni
YOO-nee

---

1. Pronounce *ü* like "ee" with your lips in a tight circle.
2. *kh* is a guttural sound.
3. Stress the syllables in capital letters.

July	August	September
Juli	August	September
YOO-lee	*ow-GOOST*	*zep-TEM-ber*

October	November	December
Oktober	November	Dezember
ohk-TOH-ber	*no-VEM-ber*	*day-TS'EM-ber*

What date?
Welches Datum?
VEL-khess DA-toom?

on the first of March
am ersten März
ahm AIR-sten mairts

on the second . . .
am zweiten . . .
ahm TS'VY-ten . . .

third . . .
dritten . . .
DRIT-ten . . .

fourth of March.
vierten März.
FEER-ten mairts.

on the 25th of December
am fünfundzwanzigsten
   Dezember
*ahm fünf-oont-TS'VAHN-
   ts'ikh-sten
   day-TS'EM-ber*

Merry Christmas!
Fröhliche Weihnachten!
*FRER-likh-eh
   VY-nahkh-ten!*

on the first of January
am ersten Januar
ahm AIR-sten YA-noo-ar

Happy New Year!
Glückliches Neujahr!
GLÜKH-likh-ess NOY-yar!

Today is a holiday.
Heute ist ein Feiertag.
HOY-teh isst ine FY-er-tahk.

Congratulations!
Herzliche Glückwünsche!
*HAIRTS-lik-kheh GLÜK-
   vůn-sheh!*

Best wishes on your birthday!
Alles gute zum Geburtstag!
AHL-less GOO-teh ts'oom gheh-BOORTS-tahk!

7. Money

This section contains the vocabulary necessary for changing money. The written abbreviation for the German mark is **DM,** for the Austrian schilling **Sch,** and for the Swiss franc **Fr**.

Where can I change money?
Wo kann ich Geld wechseln?
vo kahn ikh ghelt VEX-eln?

Can I change dollars here?
Kann ich hier Dollar wechseln?
kahn ikh heer DOH-lar VEX-eln?

Where is the moneychanger?
Wo ist der Geldwechsler?
vo isst dair GHELT-vex-ler?

Where is the bank?
Wo ist die Bank?
vo isst dee bahnk?

What time does the bank open?
Um wieviel Uhr öffnet die Bank?
oom VEE-feel oor ERF-net dee bahnk?

When does the bank close?
Wann schließt die Bank?
vahnn shleest dee bahnk?

What is the dollar rate?
Was ist der Dollarwert?
vahss isst dair DOH-lar-vairt?

It is three marks for one dollar.
Es ist drei Mark auf einen Dollar.
ess isst dry mark owf INE-en DOH-lar.

I want to change $50.
Ich möchte fünfzig Dollar wechseln.
ikh MERKH-teh FÜNF-ts'ikh DOH-lar VEX-eln.

---

1. Pronounce *ů* like "ee" with your lips in a tight circle.
2. *kh* is a guttural sound.
3. Stress the syllables in capital letters.

Do you accept traveler's checks?
Nehmen Sie Reiseschecks?
NAYM'en zee RYE-zeh-sheks?

Of course.	**Unfortunately not.**
Natürlich.	Leider nicht.
na-TÜR-likh.	*LY-der nikht.*

Will you accept my check?
Nehmen Sie meinen Scheck?
NAYM'en zee MY-nen shek?

Have you identification with you?
Haben Sie einen Ausweis bei sich?
HAHB'en zee INE-en OWSS-vice by zikh?

Yes indeed.	**Here is my passport.**
Jawohl.	Hier ist mein Pass.
ya-VOHL.	*heer isst mine pahss.*

Give me two fifty-mark notes.
Geben Sie mir zwei Fünfzigmarkscheine.
GAYB'en zee meer ts'vy FÜNF-ts'ikh-mark-shy-neh.

I need some small change.
Ich brauche Kleingeld.
ikh BROW-kheh KLINE-ghelt.

8. Basic Foods

The foods and drinks mentioned in this section will enable you to be well-fed in your travels in German-speaking countries. The section that follows this will deal with special regional dishes, representative of the tasty and substantial cuisine of Germany and Austria.

breakfast
das Frühstück
dahss FRÜ-shtŭk

orange juice
Orangensaft
oh-RAHN-ghen-zahft

boiled eggs
gekochte Eier
ge-KOKH-teh EYE-er

fried eggs
Spiegeleier
SHPEE-ghel-eye-er

with bacon
mit Speck
mit shpeck

with ham
mit Schinken
mit SHINK-en

an omelet
ein Omelett
ine ohm-LET

scrambled eggs
Rühreier
RÜR-eye-er

toast
Toast
toast

coffee with cream
Kaffee mit Sahne
ka-FAY mit ZA-neh

coffee with hot milk
Kaffee mit heißer Milch
ka-FAY mit HY-ser milkh

hot chocolate
heiße Schokolade
HI-seh sho-ko-LA-deh

tea with lemon
Tee mit Zitrone
teh mit ts'ee-TRO-neh

lunch
Mittagessen
MIT-tahk-ess-en

dinner
Abendessen
AH-bent-ess-en

Do you know a good restaurant?
Kennen Sie ein gutes Restaurant?
KEN'en zee ine GOOT-es reh-sto-RAHNG?

---

1. Pronounce *ŭ* like "ee" with your lips in a tight circle.
2. *kh* is a guttural sound.
3. Stress the syllables in capital letters.

A table for three.
Ein Tisch für drei.
ine tish für dry.

Follow me, please.
Folgen Sie mir, bitte.
FOLG'en zee meer, BIT-teh.

The menu, please.
Die Speisekarte, bitte.
dee SHPY-zeh-car-teh, BIT-teh.

What do you recommend?
Was können Sie empfehlen?
vahss KERN'en zee emp-FAIL'en?

What is this?
Was ist das?
vahss isst dahss?

I'll take this.
Ich nehme das.
ikh NAY-meh dahss.

First a cocktail.
Zuerst einen Cocktail.
ts'oo-EHRST INE-en cocktail.

Then an appetizer.
Dann eine Vorspeise.
dahn INE-eh FOR-shpy-zeh.

herring
Hering
HEHR-ring

salmon
Lachs
lahx

oysters
Austern
OWS-tern

lobster
Hummer
HOOM-mer

shrimp
Garnelen
gar-NEH-len

soup
Suppe
ZOOP-peh

fish
Fisch
fish

chicken
Hühnchen
HÜNT-yen

roast chicken
Hühnerbraten
HÜ-ner-bra-ten

duck
Ente
EN-teh

pork
Schweinefleisch
SHVY-neh-flysh

lamb
Lammfleisch
LAHM-flysh

roast veal
Kalbsbraten
KAHLPS-bra-ten

sausage (big)	sausage (small)	chopped steak
Wurst	Würstchen	Hackbraten
voorst	*VÜRST-yen*	*HAHK-bra-ten*

steak	rare	well done	bread
Steak	roh	gut durchgebraten	Brot
shtehk	*ro*	*goot DOORKH-gheh-brah'ten*	*broht*

butter	noodles	without . . .	with . . .
Butter	Nudeln	ohne . . .	mit . . .
BOOT-ter	*NOO-deln*	*OH-neh . . .*	*mit . . .*

vegetables	rice	green beans
Gemüse	Reis	grüne Bohnen
gheh-MÜ-zeh	*rice*	*GRÜ-neh BO-nen*

peas	spinach	carrots
Erbsen	Spinat	Karotten
ERP-sen	*shpin-AHT*	*ka-ROHT-ten*

cabbage	tomatoes	onions
Kohl	Tomaten	Zwiebeln
kohl	*toh-MA-ten*	*TS'VEE-beln*

mushrooms	asparagus	garlic
Pilze	Spargel	Knoblauch
PIL-ts'eh	*SHPAR-ghel*	*K'NOB-l'owkh*

fried potatoes	boiled potatoes	mashed potatoes
Bratkartoffeln	Salzkartoffeln	Kartoffelpüree
BRAHT-kar-toff-eln	*ZAHLTS-kar-toff-eln*	*kar-TOFF-el-pü-ray*

---

1. Pronounce *ü* like "ee" with your lips in a tight circle.
2. *kh* is a guttural sound.
3. Stress the syllables in capital letters.

potato salad	salad	oil
Kartoffelsalat	Salat	Öl
kar-TOFF-el-za-laht	*za-LAHT*	*erl*

vinegar	salt	pepper	mustard
Essig	Salz	Pfeffer	Senf
ESS-ikh	*zahlts*	*PFEF-er*	*zenf*

What wine do you recommend?
Welchen Wein empfehlen Sie?
VEL-khen vine emp-FAIL'en zee?

white wine	red wine
Weißwein	Rotwein
VICE-vine	*ROHT-vine*

beer	light beer	dark beer
Bier	helles Bier	dunkles Bier
beer	*HELL-ess beer*	*DOONK-less beer*

champagne	To your health!
Sekt	Prosit!
zekt	*PRO-zit!*

fruit	grapes	peaches
Obst	Weintrauben	Pfirsiche
ohpst	*VINE-tr'ow-ben*	*PFEER-zikh-eh*

apples	pears	bananas
Äpfel	Birnen	Bananen
EHP-fel	*BEER-nen*	*ba-NA-nen*

pineapples	strawberries	oranges
Ananas	Erdbeeren	Apfelsinen
ah-na-NAHSS	*AIRD-bair-en*	*ahp-fel-ZEE-nen*

For dessert:	cake	pastry	cheese
Zum Nachtisch:	Kuchen	Gebäck	Käse
ts'oom NAHKH-tish:	*KOO-khen*	*gheh-BAKE*	*KAY-zeh*

ice cream	**coffee**	**expresso**
Eiscreme	Kaffee	Expresso
ICE-kreh-meh	*ka-FAY*	*expresso*

More, please.	**That's enough, thank you.**
Mehr, bitte.	Das ist genug, danke.
mair, BIT-teh.	*dahss isst gheh-NOOK, DAHN-keh.*

Waiter!	**Waitress!**	**The check, please.**
Herr Ober!	Fräulein!	Die Rechnung, bitte.
hair OH-ber!	*FROY-line!*	*dee REKH-noong, BIT-teh.*

Is the tip included?
Ist das Trinkgeld einbegriffen?
isst dahss TRINK-ghelt INE-beh-griff'en?

I think the bill is incorrect.
Ich glaube, die Rechnung stimmt nicht.
ikh GL'OW-beh, dee REKH-noong shtimt nikht.

Oh, no, sir . . .	**look here . . .**	**. . . you see?**
Aber nein, mein	schauen Sie	. . . sehen Sie?
Herr . . .	her . . .	. . . ZAY'en zee?
AH-ber nine, mine	*SH'OW'en zee*	
hair . . .	*hair . . .*	

Yes, that's right.	**It's okay.**
Ja, das ist richtig.	Das ist in Ordnung.
ya, dahss isst RIKH-tikh.	*dahss isst in ORD-noong.*

Come again soon.
Kommen Sie bald wieder.
KOHM'en zee bahlt VEE-der.

---

1. Pronounce *ü* like "ee" with your lips in a tight circle.
2. *kh* is a guttural sound.
3. Stress the syllables in capital letters.

POINT TO THE ANSWER

When you are at a restaurant and you wish to make sure that you understand the menu, show the following section to the waiter so that he or she can select the answer. The sentence in German after the arrow asks him or her to point to the answer.

> ➡ *Zeigen Sie bitte hierunter Ihr Antwort auf meine Frage. Vielen Dank.*

Dies ist unser Spezialität.
This is our specialty.

Es ist fertig.
It's ready.

Es ist nicht fertig.
It isn't ready.

Es dauert _____ Minuten.
It takes _____ minutes.

Wir haben das heute nicht.
We don't have it today.

Es wird nur Freitags serviert.
It is served only on Fridays.

Es ist
It is

Hühnchen,
chicken,

Schweinefleisch,
pork,

Lammfleisch,
lamb,

Kalbfleisch,
veal,

Rindfleisch,
beef,

Wurst,
sausage,

Schinken,
ham,

Haase,
rabbit,

Fisch.
fish.

. . . mit Gemüsen.
. . . with vegetables.

. . . mit einer Soße.
. . . with a sauce.

9. Food Specialties of Germany and Austria

Knowing the names of special dishes will be useful in restaurants or private homes where you may be invited. These dishes commonly appear on most German menus and are so much a part of German and Austrian dining tradition that you should recognize them and know how to pronounce them as well as to enjoy them. We have written the German first, since this is how you will see it on the menu.

Gulaschsuppe
GOO-lahsh ZOOP-eh
veal soup with spices

Ochsenschwanzsuppe
OX-en shvahnts-zoop-eh
oxtail soup

Gemischter Aufschnitt
gheh-MISH-ter OWF-shnit
mixed cold cuts

Gekochte Rinderbrust
gheh-KOHK-teh RIN-der-broost
boiled brisket of beef

Hasenpfeffer
HA-zen-pfef-fer
rabbit stewed in vinegar and pepper

Schweinepfeffer mit Knödeln
SHVINE-eh-pfef-fer mit K'NER-deln
spiced pork with dumplings

Rippchen mit Sauerkraut
RIP-khen mit Z'OW-er-kr'owt
pork chops with sauerkraut

---

1. Pronounce *ů* like "ee" with your lips in a tight circle.
2. *kh* is a guttural sound.
3. Stress the syllables in capital letters.

Bauernschmaus
B'OW-ern-shm'owss
smoked ham, sausages, pork, and dumplings with
  sauerkraut

Sauerbraten mit Rotkohl
Z'OW-er bra-ten mit ROHT-kohl
pot roast with red cabbage

Eintopfgericht
INE-tohpf-gheh-rikht
casserole of meat and vegetables

Nierenbraten
NEER-en bra-ten
roast loin of veal with kidneys

Schweinebraten
SH'VY-neh-bra-ten
roast pork

Würstelbraten
VÜR-stel-bra-ten
roast beef with sausages

Geräucherter Rheinlachs
gheh-ROY-kher-ter RINE-lahx
smoked salmon from the Rhine

Sülze
ZÜL-ts'eh
meat in aspic

Blutwurst
BLOOT-voorst
blood sausage

Leberwurst
LAY-ber-voorst
liver sausage

Bratwurst
BRAHT-voorst
pork sausage

Wiener Würstchen
VEE-ner VÜRST-yen
"hot dogs"

Weißwurst
VICE-voorst
white veal sausage

Kartoffelpuffer
kar-TOFF-el-poof-er
potato pancakes

Lebkuchen
LAIP-koo-khen
spice cake

Doboschtorte
DOH-bosh-tort-eh
seven-layer cake with mocha cream

Sachertorte
ZA-kher-tort-eh
chocolate cake with whipped cream

How do you like it?
Wie schmeckt es Ihnen?
vee shmekt ess EEN-en?

It's delicious!
Es ist sehr schmackhaft!
ess isst zair SHMAHK-hahft!

It's excellent!
Ausgezeichnet!
OWSS-gheh-ts'eye-khnet!

My congratulations to the chef!
Ich gratuliere dem Koch!
ikh grah-too-LEER-eh dem kohkh!

Thank you for a wonderful dinner.
Danke sehr für ein wunderbares Abendessen!
DAHN-keh zair für ine voon-der-BAR-ess AH-bent-ess'en!

You are welcome.
Bitte schön.
BIT-teh shern.

I'm happy you enjoyed it.
Es freut mich, dass es Ihnen geschmeckt hat.
ess froyt mikh, dahss ess EEN-en ghe-shmehkt haht.

---

1. Pronounce *ů* like "ee" with your lips in a tight circle.
2. *kh* is a guttural sound.
3. Stress the syllables in capital letters.

10. Transportation

Getting around by public transportation is enjoyable not only for the new and interesting things you see but also because of the opportunities you have for practicing German. To make your travels easier use short phrases when speaking to drivers or others when you ask directions. And don't forget **Bitte** and **Danke**!

Bus

Bus
Autobus
OW-toh-booss

Where is the bus stop?
Wo ist die Bushaltestelle?
vo isst dee BOOSS-hahl-teh-shtel-leh?

Do you go to the Railroad Terminal Square?
Fahren Sie zum Bahnhofplatz?
FAR'en zee ts'oom BAHN-hohf-plahtz?

No. Take number nine.
Nein. Nehmen Sie die Nummer neun.
nine. NAYM'en zee dee NOOM-er noyn.

How much is the fare?
Was kostet die Fahrt?
vahss KO-stet dee fahrt?

Where do you want to go?
Wo wollen Sie hin?
vo VOHL'en zee hin?

To the cathedral.
Zum Dom.
ts'oom dohm.

Is it far?
Ist es weit?
isst ess vite?

---

1. Pronounce *ü* like "ee" with your lips in a tight circle.
2. *kh* is a guttural sound.
3. Stress the syllables in capital letters.

No. It's near.
Nein. Es ist in der Nähe.
nine. ess isst in dair NAY-eh.

Please tell me where to get off.
Bitte sagen Sie mir, wo ich aussteigen muß.
BIT-teh ZAHG'en zee meer, vo ikh OWSS-shtyg'en mooss.

Get off here.
Steigen Sie hier aus.
SHTYG'en zee heer OWSS.

POINT TO THE ANSWER

Show the following section to a German-speaking person so he or she can select the answer. The sentence in German after the arrow asks him or her to point to the answer.

 Zeigen Sie bitte hierunter Ihr Antwort auf meine Frage. Vielen Dank.

Dort drüben.   **In dieser Richtung.**   **Ich weiß nicht.**
Over there.   In this direction.   I don't know.

Auf der anderen Seite der Straße.   **An der Ecke.**
On the other side of the street.   At the corner.

Nach rechts.   **Nach links.**   **Immer geradeaus.**
To the right.   To the left.   Straight ahead.

Taxi

Taxi!
Taxi!
tahk-see!

Are you free?
Sind Sie frei?
zint zee fry?

To this address.
Zu dieser Adresse.
ts'oo DEE-zer ah-DRESS-eh.

Do you know where it is?
Wissen Sie, wo das ist?
VISS'en zee, vo dahss isst?

I am in a hurry.
Ich bin in Eile.
ikh bin in EYE-leh.

Go fast!
Fahren Sie schnell!
FAR'en zee shnel!

Slow down!
Fahren Sie langsamer!
FAR'en zee LAHNG-zah-mer!

Stop here.
Halten Sie hier.
HAHLT'en zee heer.

At the corner.
An der Ecke.
ahn dair EHK-eh.

Wait for me.
Warten Sie auf mich.
VART'en zee owf mikh.

Okay?
Einverstanden?
INE-fair-shtahn-den?

I'll be back soon.
Ich komme gleich zurück.
Ikh KOHM-eh glykh
  ts'oo-RÜK.

In five minutes.
In fünf Minuten.
in fünf mee-NOOT-en.

How much is it per hour?
Was kostet es pro Stunde?
*vahss KO-stet ess pro
  SHTOON-deh?*

. . . per kilometer?
. . . der Kilometer?
. . . dair kee-lo-MAYT-er?

---

1. Pronounce ü like "ee" with your lips in a tight circle.
2. *kh* is a guttural sound.
3. Stress the syllables in capital letters.

What's the matter?	**After midnight there's a surcharge.**
Was ist los?	Nach Mitternacht ist ein Zuschlag.
vahss isst lohss?	*Nahkh MIT-ter-nahkht isst ine*
	TS'OO-shlahg.

POINT TO THE ANSWER

To make sure that you understand the taxi driver's answer to your question, show him or her the following section so he or she can select the answer. The sentence in German after the arrow asks him or her to point to the answer.

 Zeigen Sie bitte hierunter Ihr Antwort auf meine Frage. Vielen Dank.

Ich warte auf Sie hier.
I will wait for you here.

Ich kann nicht warten.
I can't wait.

Ich kann hier nicht parken.
I can't park here.

Ich komme zurück um Sie abzuholen.
I'll be back to pick you up.

Das ist nicht genug.	**Das Gepäck ist extra.**
It's not enough.	The baggage is extra.

Subway

Is there a subway in this city?
Gibt es in dieser Stadt eine U-Bahn?
ghipt ess in DEE-zer shtaht INE-eh OO-bahn?

Where is the subway?
Wo ist die U-Bahn?
vo isst dee OO-bahn?

What is the fare?
Wieviel ist der Fahrpreis?
vee-FEEL isst dehr FAR-price?

   U-Bahn is short for **Untergrundbahn**—"underground railroad."

Train

Where is the railroad station?
Wo ist der Bahnhof?
vo isst dair BAHN-hohf?

Where do I buy tickets?
Wo kann ich Fahrkarten kaufen?
vo kahn ikh FAR-kar-ten KOW-fen?

One ticket for Munich.
Eine Fahrkarte nach München.
INE-eh FAR-kar-teh nahkh MÜNT-yen.

---

1. Pronounce *ů* like "ee" with your lips in a tight circle.
2. *kh* is a guttural sound.
3. Stress the syllables in capital letters.

Round trip.	One way.	A timetable.
Hin- und Rückfahrt.	Nur einfach.	Ein Fahrplan.
hin oont RŮK-fahrt.	*noor INE-fakh.*	*ine FAR-plahn.*

First class.	Second class.
Erste Klasse.	Zweite Klasse.
EHRST-eh KLAHSS-eh.	*TS'VY-teh KLAHSS-eh.*

Where is the train for Cologne?
Wo ist der Zug nach Köln?
vo isst der ts'ook nakh Kerln?

When do we leave?	Is this seat taken?
Wann fahren wir ab?	Ist dieser Platz besetzt?
vahn FAR'en veer ahp?	*isst DEE-zer plahts beh-*
	ZETST?

With your permission.	Of course.
Erlauben Sie, bitte.	Natürlich.
air-L'OW-ben zee, BIT-teh.	*na-TŮR-likh.*

At what time do we arrive in Hamburg?
Um wieviel Uhr kommen wir in Hamburg an?
oom VEE-feel oor KOHM'en veer in HAHM-boorg ahn?

Does the train stop in Bremen?
Hält der Zug in Bremen?
hehlt dair ts'ook in BRAY-men?

How long does the train stop here?
Wie lange hält der Zug hier?
vee LAHNG-eh hehlt dair ts'ook heer?

Where is the dining car?
Wo ist der Speisewagen?
vo isst dair SHPY-zeh-va-ghen?

I can't find my ticket.
Ich kann meine Fahrkarte nicht finden.
ikh kahn MINE-eh FAR-kar-teh nikht FIN-den.

Wait.
Warten Sie.
VART'en zee.

Here it is.
Hier ist sie.
heer isst zee.

Can you help me?
Können Sie mir helfen?
KERN'en zee meer HELF'en?

I took the wrong train.
Ich habe nicht den richtigen Zug genommen.
ikh HAHB-eh nikht den RIKH-tee-ghen ts'ook ghe-NOHM'en.

I'd like to go to Berlin.
Ich möchte gern nach Berlin fahren.
ikh MERKH-teh gairn nakh bair-LEEN FAR'en.

POINT TO THE ANSWER

To make sure that you understand the answer to questions, show the following section to the conductor or station guard so he or she can select the answer. The sentence in German after the arrow asks him or her to point to the answer.

 Zeigen Sie bitte hierunter Ihr Antwort auf meine Frage. Vielen Dank.

Bahnsteig Nummer _____ .
Track number _____ .

---

1. Pronounce *ü* like "ee" with your lips in a tight circle.
2. *kh* is a guttural sound.
3. Stress the syllables in capital letters.

Unten.	Oben.	In dieser Richtung.
Downstairs.	Upstairs.	That way.

Der Zug geht in _____ Minuten.
The train leaves in _____ minutes.

Dies ist nicht Ihr Zug.	**Er geht nach _____ .**
This is not your train.	It goes to _____ .

Sie müssen in _____ umsteigen.
You must change at _____ .

Wir kommen um _____ Uhr an.
We arrive at _____ o'clock.

Ship

What time does the ship sail?
Um wieviel Uhr fahrt das Schiff ab?
oom VEE-feel oor fahrt dahss shif ahp?

From which pier?
Von welcher Anlegestelle?
fohn VEL-kher AHN-leh-gheh-shtel-eh?

Where is my cabin?
Wo ist meine Kabine?
vo isst MINE-eh ka-BEE-neh?

Where is my luggage?	**. . . the purser?**
Wo ist mein Gepäck?	. . . der Zahlmeister?
vo isst mine gheh-PAYK?	*. . . dair TS'AHL-my-ster?*

Where is . . .	**. . . the swimming pool?**	**. . . the bar?**
Wo ist . . .	. . . das Schwimmbad?	. . . die Bar?
vo isst . . .	*. . . dahss SHVIM-baht?*	*. . . dee bar?*

. . . the movie?
. . . das Kino?
. . . *dahss KEE-no?*

. . . the dining salon?
. . . der Speisesaal?
. . . *dair SHPY-zeh-zahl?*

yacht	launch	sailboat
Jacht	Barkasse	Segelboot
yahkht	*BAR-kas-seh*	*ZEH-ghel-boat*

first class	tourist class
erste Klasse	Touristenklasse
ehrst-eh KLAHSS-eh	*too-RIST-en-klahss-eh*

ferry	Rhine steamboat
Fähre	Rheindampfer
FAIR-eh	*RINE-dahmp-fer.*

---

1. Pronounce *ů* like "ee" with your lips in a tight circle.
2. *kh* is a guttural sound.
3. Stress the syllables in capital letters.

11. Trips by Car

Car Rental

Where can one rent a car?
Wo kann man einen Wagen mieten?
vo kahn mahn INE-en VA-ghen MEET'en?

Where can one . . .   . . . rent a motorcycle?
Wo kann man . . .   . . . ein Motorrad mieten?
vo kahn mahn . . .   . . . ine MO-tohr-raht MEET'en?

. . . rent a bicycle?
. . . ein Fahrrad mieten?
. . . ine FAR-raht MEET'en?

I want to rent a car.
Ich möchte einen Wagen mieten.
ikh MERKH-teh INE-en VA-ghen MEET'en.

How much per day?
Vieviel kostet es pro Tag?
vee-FEEL KO-stet ess pro tahk?

How much per kilometer?*
Wieviel pro Kilometer?
vee-FEEL pro kee-lo-MAY-ter?

Is the gasoline included?
Ist Benzin mit einbegriffen?
isst ben-TS'EEN mit INE-beh-griff'en?

---

1. Pronounce ů like "ee" with your lips in a tight circle.
2. *kh* is a guttural sound.
3. Stress the syllables in capital letters.

---

* Distances are reckoned in kilometers, approximately ⅝ of a mile.

Is the transmission automatic?
Hat der Wagen eine automatische Schaltung?
haht der VA-ghen INE-eh ow-toh-MA-tish-eh SHAHL-toong?

I would like to try it out.
Ich würde ihn gerne ausprobieren.
ikh VÛR-deh een GAIRN-eh OWSS-pro-beer'en.

Gas Station

Where is the next gas station?
Wo ist die nächste Tankstelle?
vo isst dee NAIKH-steh TAHNK-shtel-eh?

How much per liter?*
Was Kostet der Liter?
vahss KO-stet dair LEE-ter?

Thirty liters, please.
Dreißig Liter, bitte.
DRY-sikh LEE-ter, BIT-teh.

Fill up the tank.
Machen Sie den Tank voll.
MAHKH'en zee den tahnk fohl.

Please check whether . . .   **. . . the tires . . .**
Bitte sehen Sie nach, ob . . .   . . . die Reifen . . .
BIT-teh ZAY'en zee nahkh,   *. . . dee RYE-fen . . .*
  ohp . . .

. . . the sparkplugs . . .   **. . . the brakes . . .**
. . . die Zündkerzen . . .   . . . die Bremsen . . .
. . . dee TS'ÛNT-kair-ts'en . . .   *. . . dee BREM-zen . . .*

---

* Gas is sold by the liter—1.05 quarts; four liters make approximately one gallon.

. . . are okay.
. . . in Ordnung sind.
. . . in ORD-noong zint.

Please check whether . . .
Bitte sehen Sie nach, ob . . .
BIT-teh ZAY'en zee nahkh,
  ohp . . .

. . . the water . . .
. . . das Wasser . . .
. . . dahss VAHSS-er . . .

. . . the oil . . .
. . . das Öl . . .
. . . dahss erl . . .

. . . the carbuertor . . .
. . . der Vergaser . . .
. . . dair fair-GA-zer . . .

. . . the battery . . .
. . . die Batterie . . .
. . . dee ba-teh-REE . . .

. . . is okay.
. . . in Ordnung ist.
. . . in ORD-noong isst.

Change the oil, please.
Ölwechsel, bitte.
ERL-vex-el, BIT-teh.

Change this tire.
Wechseln Sie diesen Reifen.
VEX-eln zee DEE-zen
  RYE-fen.

The car needs a grease job.
Der Wagen braucht Schmierung.
dair VA-ghen browkht SHMEER-oong.

Wash the car.
Waschen Sie den Wagen.
VA-shen zee den VA-ghen.

A road map, please.
Eine Straßenkarte, bitte.
INE-eh SHTRA-sen-kar-teh, BIT-teh.

---

1. Pronounce *ů* like "ee" with your lips in a tight circle.
2. *kh* is a guttural sound.
3. Stress the syllables in capital letters.

Asking Directions

Where does this road lead?
Wohin Führt diese Straße?
vo-HIN fürt DEE-zeh SHTRAHSS-eh?

Is this the way to Frankfurt?
Geht es hier nach Frankfurt?
gayt ess heer nahkh FRAHNK-foort?

Is the road good?
Ist die Straße gut?
isst dee SHTRAHSS-eh goot?

Which is the highway to Stuttgart?
Welche Autobahn führt nach Stuttgart?
VEL-kheh OW-toh-bahn fürt nahkh SHTOOT-gart?

In this direction.
In dieser Richtung.
in DEE-zer RIKH-toong.

Is the next town far?
Ist die nächste Stadt weit?
isst dee NAYK-steh shtaht vite?

Is there a good restaurant there?
Gibt es dort ein gutes Restaurant?
gibt ess dort ine GOO-tess reh-sto-RAHNG?

. . . a good hotel?
. . . ein gutes Hotel?
. . . ine GOO-tess ho-TEL?

What is it called?
Wie heißt es?
vee hice'st ess?

POINT TO THE ANSWER

To make sure that you understand the answer to your questions about driving directions, show the following section to the person whom you are asking. The sentence in German after the arrow asks him or her to point to the answer.

 Zeigen Sie bitte hierunter Ihr Antwort auf meine Frage. Vielen Dank.

Es heißt _____ .
It's called _____ .

Folgen Sie dieser Straße.
Follow this road.

Ungefähr fünfzig Kilometer.
About fifty kilometers.

Auf dieser Landkarte sind Sie hier.
You are here on this map.

Biegen Sie rechts ab am Kreuzweg
Turn right at the crossroads.

An der Ampel, links.
At the traffic signal, left.

Sie überqueren die Brüche.
Cross the bridge.

Immer gerade aus.
Go straight ahead.

---

1. Pronounce *ŭ* like "ee" with your lips in a tight circle.
2. *kh* is a guttural sound.
3. Stress the syllables in capital letters.

Fahren Sie auf die Autobahn.
Get on the Autobahn.

Aber Vorsicht!
But be careful!

Es gibt eine Gechwindigskeitbegrenzung.
There's a speed limit.

Emergencies and Repairs

Your license, please!
Ihren Führerschein, bitte!
EER-en FÜR-air-shine,
BIT-teh!

Here it is, sir.
Hier ist er, mein Herr.
heer isst air, mine hair.

And the car registration.
Und die Kraftfahrkarte.
oont dee KRAHFT-far-kar-teh.

It wasn't my fault.
Es war nicht meine Schuld.
ess var nikht MINE-eh schoolt.

The truck skidded.
Der Lastwagen kam ins Schleudern.
dair LAHST-va-ghen kahm ins SHLOY-dern.

The fool crashed into me!
Der Dummkopf fuhr in mich hinein!
dair DOOM-kopf foor mikh hin-INE!

As German drivers are inclined to be rather competitive—
and fast—words like **Dummkopf** (literally, "dumbhead"),
Ochse ("ox"), **Idiot,** etc., are frequent and rather mild ex-
pletives. However, self-control and good humor, plus a dip-
lomatic use of German, will make driving safe and
enjoyable.

I am having difficulties.
Ich habe Schwierigkeiten.
ikh HAHB-eh SHVEE-rikh-kite-en.

My car has broken down.
Mein Wagen ist kaputt.
mine VA-ghen isst ka-POOT.

Can you help me?
Können Sie mir helfen?
KERN'en zee meer HELF'en?

I have a flat tire.
Ich habe eine Panne.
ikh HAHB-eh INE-eh PA-neh.

Can you lend me a jack?
Können Sie mir einen Wagenheber leihen?
KERN'en zee meer INE-en VA-ghen-hay-ber LIE'en?

It's stuck.
Er sitzt fest.
air zitst fest.

Can you push me?
Können Sie mich schieben?
KERN'en zee mikh SHEE-ben?

Thank you very much.
Vielen Dank.
FEEL-en dahnk.

You are very kind.
Sie sind sehr liebenswürdig.
zee zint zair LEE-bens-vůr-dikh.

I want to speak to the mechanic.
Ich möchte den Mechaniker sprechen.
ikh MERKH-teh den meh-KHA-nik-er SHPREKH'en.

The car doesn't go well.
Der Wagen läuft nicht gut.
dair VA-ghen loyft nikht goot.

---

1. Pronounce ů like "ee" with your lips in a tight circle.
2. *kh* is a guttural sound.
3. Stress the syllables in capital letters.

What's the matter?
Was ist los?
vahss isst lohss?

The motor is making a funny noise.
Der Motor macht ein eigenartiges Geräusch.
*dair MO-tor mahkht ine EYE-ghen-art-ig-ess
   gheh-ROYSH.*

It's difficult to start.
Er ist schwierig zu starten.
air isst SHVEE-rikh ts'oo SHTART'en.

Can you fix it?
Können Sie es reparieren?
KERN'en zee ess ray-pa-REER'en?

What will it cost?
Was wird es kosten?
vahss veert ess KO-sten?

How long will it take?
Wie lange wird es dauern?
vee LAHNG-eh veert ess DOW-ern?

I'm in a hurry.
Ich bin in Eile.
ikh bin in EYE-leh.

POINT TO THE ANSWER

To make sure that you understand the answer to questions
about car repair, show the following section to the mechanic
so he or she can select the answer. The sentence in German
after the arrow asks him or her to point to the answer.

Zeigen Sie bitte hierunter Ihr Antwort auf meine Frage. Vielen Dank.

Heute ist es nicht möglich.
Today isn't possible.

Vielleicht dieser Abend.
Perhaps this evening.

Morgen.   **Übermorgen.**
Tomorrow.   The day after tomorrow.

Das wird Sie _____ Mark kosten.
It will cost you _____ marks.

Es wird in _____ Tagen fertig sein.
It will be ready in _____ days.

Wir haben nicht den Bestandteil.
We don't have the part.

Wir können das vorübergehend reparieren.
We can repair it temporarily.

Sie brauchen auch ein neues Reifen.
You also need a new tire.

---

1. Pronounce *ǔ* like "ee" with your lips in a tight circle.
2. *kh* is a guttural sound.
3. Stress the syllables in capital letters.

International Road Signs

Danger

Caution

Sharp turn

Crossroads

Right curve

Left curve

Guarded RR crossing

Unguarded RR crossing

Main road ahead

Bumps

One way

Do not enter

No parking

Parking

In addition, you will see or hear the following instructions:

RECHTS FAHREN
rekhts FAR'en
Keep to the right

UMLEITUNG
OOM-lye-toong
Detour

EINBAHNSTRASSE
INE-bahn-shtrahss-eh
One way

KREUZUNG
KROY-ts'oong
Crossroads

HÖCHSTGESCHWINDIGKEIT 100 KM.
HERKST-ghe-shvin-dikh-kite HOON-dert
   kee-LO-may-ter
Maximum speed 100 kilometers per hour

PARKEN VERBOTEN
PARK-en fair-BO-ten
No parking

AUTOBAHN EINFAHRT
OW-toh-bahn INE-fahrt
Autobahn entrance

AUSFAHRT
OWSS-fahrt
Exit

GESPERRT
gheh-SHPAIRT
Road closed

---

1. Pronounce *ů* like "ee" with your lips in a tight circle.
2. *kh* is a guttural sound.
3. Stress the syllables in capital letters.

12. Sight-seeing and Photography

We have combined these two important sections, since you will want to take pictures of what you are seeing. If you are taking pictures indoors, be sure to ask the custodian **Ist es erlaubt?**—"Is it permitted?"

Sight-seeing

I need a guide.
Ich brauche einen Reiseführer.
ikh BROW-kheh INE-en RYE-zeh-für-er.

Are you a guide?
Sind Sie ein Reiseführer?
zint zee ine RYE-zeh-für-er?

Do you speak English?
Sprechen Sie Englisch?
SHPREKH'en zee EHNG-lish?

It doesn't matter.
Es macht nichts.
ess mahkht nikhts.

I speak a little German.
Ich spreche ein wenig Deutsch.
ikh SHPREKH-eh ine VAY-nikh doytch.

Do you have a car?
Haben Sie einen Wagen?
HAHB'en zee INE-en VA-ghen?

---

1. Pronounce *ü* like "ee" with your lips in a tight circle.
2. *kh* is a guttural sound.
3. Stress the syllables in capital letters.

What do you charge per hour?
Was kostet es pro Stunde?
vahss KO-stet ess pro SHTOON-deh?

How much per day?
Wieviel pro Tag?
vee-FEEL pro tahk?

For two people.
Für zwei Personen.
für ts'vy pair-ZOHN-en.

A group of four.
Eine Gruppe von vier.
INE-eh GROOP-eh fohn feer.

We want to see the old part of the city.
Wir möchten die Altstadt sehen.
veer MERKHT'en dee AHLT-shtaht ZAY'en.

Where is the railroad terminal?
Wo ist der Bahnhof?
vo isst dair BAHN-hohf?

We want to go . . .   **. . . to the museum.**
Wir wollen . . .   . . . ins Museum gehen
veer VOHL'en . . .   *. . . ins moo-ZAY-oom GAY'en.*

. . . to the park.
. . . in den Park gehen.
. . . in den park GAY'en.

. . . to the Town Hall.
. . . zum Rathaus gehen.
. . . ts'oom RAHT-howss GAY'en.

. . . to the zoo.   **. . . to the market.**
. . . zum Zoo gehen.   . . . zum Markt gehen.
. . . ts'oom ts'oh GAY'en.   *. . . ts'oom markt GAY'en.*

. . . to the Hofbrau.
. . . zum Hofbräuhaus gehen.
. . . ts'oom HOHF-broy-howss GAY'en.

Observe that **gehen**—"to go"—comes at the end of the phrase, not at the beginning, as in English. When two verbs are used together, the second one, which is in the form of an infinitive or a participle, regularly comes at the end.

We want to take a trip around the city.
Wir möchten eine Stadtrundfahrt machen.
veer MERKH-ten INE-eh STAHT-roont-fahrt MAKH'en.

How beautiful!
Wie schön!
vee shern!

Very interesting!
Sehr interessant!
zair in-teh-reh-SAHNT!

From what period is this?
Aus welcher Zeit stammt dies?
owss VEL-kher ts'ite shtahmt deess?

Do you know a good cabaret?
Kennen Sie ein gutes Kabarett?
KEN'en zee ine GOOT-es ka-ba-RAY?

Let's go!
Gehen wir!
GAY'en veer!

You are a very good guide.
Sie sind ein guter Führer.
zee zint ine GOOT-er FÜR-er.

Come again tomorrow.
Kommen Sie morgen wieder.
KOHM'en zee MOR-ghen VEE-der.

At nine o'clock.
Um neun Uhr.
oom noÿn oor.

And, if you don't have a guide:

---

1. Pronounce *ü* like "ee" with your lips in a tight circle.
2. *kh* is a guttural sound.
3. Stress the syllables in capital letters.

May one enter?
Darf man eintreten?
darf mahn INE-trayt'en?

It is open.	**It is closed.**
Es ist geöffnet.	Es ist geschlossen.
ess isst gheh-ERF-net.	*ess isst gheh-SHLOSS'en.*

It opens at two o'clock.
Es wird um zwei Uhr geöffnet.
ess veert oom ts'vy oor gheh-ERF-net.

What are the visiting hours?
Wann sind die Besuchszeiten?
vahn zint dee beh-ZOOKHS-ts'y-ten?

It is closed for repairs.
Wegen Reparaturarbeiten geschlossen.
VAY-ghen reh-pa-ra-TOOR-ar-bite'en gheh-SHLOSS'en.

Can one take photos?
Darf man photographieren?
darf mahn fo-toh-grahf-EER'en?

It is permitted.	**It is forbidden.**
Es ist erlaubt.	Es ist verboten.
ess isst air-L'OWPT.	*ess isst fair-BO-ten.*

Leave your packages in the checkroom.
Lassen Sie ihr Gepäck in der Garderobe.
LAHSS'en zee eer gheh-PAYK in dair gar-deh-RO-beh.

Leave your camera here.
Lassen Sie Ihre Kamera hier.
LAHSS'en zee EER-eh KA-meh-ra heer.

What is the admission?	**One mark.**
Was kostet der Eintritt?	Eine Mark.
vahss KO-stet dair INE-trit?	*INE-eh mark.*

And for children?
Und für Kinder?
oont für KIN-der?

The admission is free.
Der Eintritt ist frei.
dair INE-trit isst fry.

Your ticket, please!
Ihre Eintrittskarte, bitte!
EER-eh INE-trits-kar-teh, BIT-teh!

Follow me!
Folgen Sie mir!
FOLG'en zee meer!

No smoking.
Rauchen verboten.
R'OWKH'en fair-BO-ten.

This way, please!
Hierher, bitte!
HEER-hair, BIT-teh!

This castle . . .
Diese Burg . . .
DEE-zeh boork . . .

This palace . . .
Dieses Schloß . . .
DEE-zehss shloss . . .

This church . . .
Diese Kirche . . .
DEE-zeh KEER-kheh . . .

This monument . . .
Dieses Denkmal . . .
*DEE-zehss
    DEHNK-mahl . . .*

This street . . .
Diese Straße . . .
DEE-zeh SHTRAHSS-eh . . .

This square . . .
Dieser Platz . . .
DEE-zer plahtz . . .

. . . is very interesting.
. . . ist sehr interessant.
. . . isst zair in-teh-reh-SAHNT.

It's magnificent!
Es ist großartig!
ess isst GROSS-art-ikh!

---

1. Pronounce *ů* like "ee" with your lips in a tight circle.
2. *kh* is a guttural sound.
3. Stress the syllables in capital letters.

It's very old, isn't it?
Es ist sehr alt, nicht wahr?
ess isst zair ahlt, nikht vahr?

This is for you.
Das ist für Sie.
dahss isst fûr zee.

Some signs you may see in public places:

HERREN   or **MÄNNER**   **DAMEN**   or **FRAUEN**
HAIR-en   *MEN-er*   *DA-men*   *FROW-en*
Gentlemen   Men   Ladies   Women

EINGANG   **AUSGANG**   **DRÜCKEN**   **ZIEHEN**
INE-gahng   *OWSS-gahng*   *DRÜK'en*   *TS'EE'en*
Entrance   Exit   Push   Pull

AUF   **ZU**   **KALT**   **WARM**   **HEISS**
owf   *ts'oo*   *kahlt*   *vahrm*   *hice*
On   Off   Cold   Warm   Hot

BESUCHSZEITEN   **AUSKUNFT**
beh-ZOOKHS-ts'y-ten   *OWSS-koonft*
Visiting hours   Information

ZUTRITT VERBOTEN   **GARDEROBE**
TS'OO-trit fair-BO-ten   *gar-deh-RO-beh*
No admission   Checkroom

RAUCHEN VERBOTEN
R'OW-khen fair-BO-ten
No smoking

   Verboten on signs has the general connotation of "No!"
or "Don't do it!"; so when you see it, don't walk on the
grass, smoke, take pictures, or whatever the case may be.

Photography

Where is a camera shop?
Wo ist ein Fotogeschäft?
vo isst ine FO-toh-gheh-sheft?

I need some film for my camera.
Ich brauche etwas Film für meinen Foto-Apparat.
ikh BROW-kheh ET-vahss film für MY-nen
   FO-toh-ah-pa-RAHT.

. . . **black-and-white.**   . . . **color film.**
. . . schwarz-weiß.   . . . Farbfilm.
. . . *shvarts-vice.*   . . . *FARP-film.*

. . . **movie film**
. . . Film für Film-Kamera.
. . . *Film für FILM-ka-meh-ra.*

This is to be developed.
Das muß entwickelt werden.
dahss mooss ent-VIK-elt VAIRD'en.

How much per print?   **Two prints of each.**
Was kostet ein Abzug?   Von jedem Bild zwei.
vahss KO-stet ine AHP-ts'ook?   *fon YAID-em bilt ts'vy.*

An enlargement.
Eine Vergrößerung.
INE-eh fair-GRER-seh-roong.

About this size.
Ungefähr diese Größe.
oon-ghe-FAIR DEE-zeh GRER-seh.

---

1. Pronounce *ů* like "ee" with your lips in a tight circle.
2. *kh* is a guttural sound.
3. Stress the syllables in capital letters.

When will it be ready?
Wann wird es fertig sein?
vahn veert ess FAIR-tikh zine?

A battery.
Eine Batterie.
EYE-neh ba-teh-REE.

For this camera.
Für diese Kamera.
für DEE-zeh KA-meh-ra.

May I take a photograph of you?
Darf ich Sie photographieren?
dahrf ikh zee fo-toh-gra-FEER'en?

Stand here, please.
Stellen Sie sich hierher, bitte.
SHTEL'en zee zikh HEER-hair, BIT-teh.

Don't move!
Nicht bewegen!
nikht beh-VAYG'en!

Smile!
Lächeln!
LAIKH'eln!

That's it.
Das wär's.
dahss vairss.

Will you please take one of me?
Würden Sie bitte eine von mir machen?
VURD'en zee BIT-teh INE-eh fohn meer MAKH'en?

In front of this.
Davor.
da-FOR.

You are very kind.
Sie sind sehr freundlich.
zee zint zair FROYND-likh.

May I send you a copy?
Darf Ich Ihnen einen Abzug senden?
darf ikh EE-nen INE-en AHP-ts'ook ZEN-den?

Your name, please?
Ihr Name, bitte?
eer NA-meh, BIT-teh?

Your address?
Ihre Adresse?
EER-eh ah-DRESS-eh?

POINT TO THE ANSWER

In making arrangements in a **Fotogeschäft,** the following answers to questions should be useful. The sentence in German after the arrow asks the sales clerk to point to the answer.

 Zeigen Sie bitte hierunter Ihr Antwort auf meine Frage. Vielen Dank.

Kommen Sie morgen zurück.	**Um _____ Uhr.**
Come back tomorrow.	At _____ o'clock.

Kommen Sie in _____ Tagen zurück.
Come back in _____ days.

Wir können es reparieren.	**Wir können es nicht reparieren.**
We can repair it.	We cannot repair it.

Wir haben keines.	**Sie können es bei _____ kriegen.**
We don't have any.	You can get it at _____ .

Asking to take pictures of someone often leads to more general conversation. For this reason the following three sections will be especially interesting to you.

---

1. Pronounce *ŭ* like "ee" with your lips in a tight circle.
2. *kh* is a guttural sound.
3. Stress the syllables in capital letters.

13. Entertainment

Things to Do

May I invite you . . .
Darf ich Sie . . .
dahrf ikh zee . . .

. . . to lunch?
. . . zum Mittagessen einladen?
. . . ts'oom MIT-tahk-ess-en INE-lahd'en?

. . . to dinner?
. . . zum Abendessen einladen?
. . . ts'oom AH-bent-ess-en INE-lahd'en?

. . . for a drink?
. . . zu einem Getränk einladen?
. . . ts'oo INE-em gheh-TRENK INE-lahd'en?

. . . for a drive?
. . . zu einer Fahrt einladen?
. . . ts'oo INE-er fahrt INE-lahd'en?

. . . to play bridge?
. . . zum Bridge einladen?
. . . ts'oom bridge INE-lahd'en?

. . . to the movies?
. . . ins Kino einladen?
. . . inss KEE-no INE-lahd'en?

. . . to the theater?
. . . ins Theater einladen?
. . . inss teh-AH-ter INE-lahd'en?

---

1. Pronounce *ü* like "ee" with your lips in a tight circle.
2. *kh* is a guttural sound.
3. Stress the syllables in capital letters.

. . . to play golf?
. . . zum Golf einladen?
. . . ts'oom gohlf INE-
  lahd'en?

. . . to play tennis?
. . . zum Tennis einladen?
. . . ts'oom TEN-nis INE-
  lahd'en?

Einladen—"to invite"—comes at the end of each sentence, in accordance with German word order.

May I ask you to dance?
Darf ich Sie um den Tanz bitten?
dahrf ikh zee oom den tahn'ts BITT'en?

Thank you very much!
Vielen Dank!
FEEL-en dahnk!

With pleasure!
Mit Vergnügen!
mit fairg-NŮ-ghen!

I am sorry.
Es tut mir leid.
ess toot meer lite.

I cannot.
Ich kann nicht.
ikh kahn nikht.

I am busy.
Ich bin beschäftigt.
ikh bin beh-SHEFT-eekht.

I am tired.
Ich bin müde.
ikh bin MŮ-deh.

I am waiting for someone.
Ich warte auf jemanden.
ikh VAR-teh owf YEH-mahn-den.

I don't feel well.
Ich fühle mich nicht gut.
ikh FŮ-leh mikh nikht goot.

Let's go . . .
Gehen wir . . .
GAY'en veer . . .

. . . to the beach.
. . . an den Strand.
. . . ahn den shtrahnt.

. . . to the meeting.
. . . zur Konferenz.
. . . ts'oor kohn-fair-ENTZ.

. . . **to a nightclub.**
. . . ins Nachtlokal.
. . . *inss NAHKHT-lo-kahl.*

. . . **to a small restaurant.**
. . . in eine Gaststätte.
. . . *in INE-eh GAHST-shtet-eh.*

. . . **to a beer hall.**
. . . in eine Bierhalle.
. . . *in INE-eh BEER-hahl-leh.*

. . . **to the movies.**
. . . ins Kino.
. . . *inss KEE-no.*

. . . **to a beer garden.**
. . . in einen Biergarten.
. . . *in INE-en BEER-gar-ten.*

Where are we going tomorrow?
Wohin gehen wir morgen?
vo-HIN GAY'en veer MOR-ghen?

Let's go . . .
Gehen wir . . .
GAY'en veer . . .

. . . **to see the town.**
. . . die Stadt anschauen.
. . . *dee shtaht AHN-sh'ow'en.*

. . . **to an art show.**
. . . zu einer Kunstausstellung.
. . . *ts'oo INE-er KOONST-owss-shtel-loong.*

---

1. Pronounce *ů* like "ee" with your lips in a tight circle.
2. *kh* is a guttural sound.
3. Stress the syllables in capital letters.

. . . to the opera.
. . . in die Oper.
. . . *in dee OH-per.*

. . . to the art museum.
. . . zum Kunstmuseum.
. . . *ts'oom KOONST-moo-zay-oom.*

. . . to the marketplace.	**. . . to the cathedral.**
. . . zum Marktplatz.	. . . zum Dom.
. . . *ts'oom MARKT-plahtz.*	. . . *ts'oom dohm.*

. . . to the old Town Hall.
. . . zum alten Rathaus.
. . . *ts'oom AHL-ten RAHT-howss.*

. . . to the harbor.	**. . . to the park.**
. . . zum Hafen.	. . . zum Park.
. . . *ts'oom HA-fen.*	. . . *ts'oom park.*

. . . to the zoo.
. . . zum Zoo.
. . . *ts'oom ts'oh.*

. . . to the observation tower.
. . . zum Aussichtsturm.
. . . *ts'oom OWSS-zikhts-toorm.*

. . . to the football game.
. . . zum Fußballspiel.
. . . *ts'oom FOOS-bahl-shpeel.*

. . . to the horse races.
. . . zum Pferderennen.
. . . *ts'oom PFAIR-deh-ren'en.*

Who is ahead?	**Come on there!**
Wer gewinnt?	Weiter so!
vair gheh-VINT?	*VY-tehr zo!*

Theaters and Nightclubs

Let's go to the theater.
Gehen wir ins Theater.
GAY'en veer inss teh-AH-ter.

Two seats, please!
Zwei Plätze, bitte!
ts'vy PLET-seh, BIT-teh!

Orchestra.
Parkett.
par-KET.

Balcony.
Balkon.
bahl-KOHN.

Are they good seats?
Sind es gute Plätze?
sint ess GOO-teh PLET-seh?

When does it start?
Wann fängt es an?
vahn fengt ess ahn?

Reserve two seats for me, please.
Reservieren Sie, bitte, zwei Plätze für mich.
reh-zehr-VEE-ren zee, BIT-teh, ts'vy PLET-seh für mikh.

Who is playing the lead?
Wer spielt die Hauptrolle?
vair shpeelt dee HOWPT-roll-eh?

She is beautiful.
Sie ist schön.
zee isst shern.

---

1. Pronounce *ů* like "ee" with your lips in a tight circle.
2. *kh* is a guttural sound.
3. Stress the syllables in capital letters.

How do you like it?
Wie gefällt es Ihnen?
vee geh-FELT ess EEN-en?

Very good!
Sehr gut!
zair goot!

It's great!
Es ist großartig!
ess isst GROSS-ar-tikh!

It's very amusing.
Es ist sehr amüsant.
ess isst zair ah-mů-ZAHNT.

Is it already over?
Schon zu Ende?
shohn ts'oo EN-deh?

And now let's go dance.
Und jetzt gehen wir tanzen.
oont yetzt GAY'en veer TAHN-ts'en.

A table near the dance floor, please.
Einen Tisch nahe der Tanzdiele, bitte.
INE-en tish NA-eh der TAHNTS-dee-leh, BIT-eh.

Shall we dance?
Wollen wir tanzen?
VOL'en veer TAHNTS'en?

Shall we stay a little while?
Wollen wir noch bleiben?
VOHL'en veer nohkh BLY-ben?

Shall we go?
Wollen wir gehen?
VOHL'en veer GAY'en?

Invitations to Dinner

Can you come for dinner at our house?
Können Sie zum Abendessen zu uns kommen?
*KERN'en zee ts'oom AH'bent-ess-en ts'oo oons
    KOHM'en?*

. . . Monday at eight?
. . . Montag, um acht?
. . . MOHN-tahk, oom akht?

With great pleasure!
Mit großem Vergnügen!
mit GROSS-em fairg-NŮG-en!

If it isn't inconvenient for you.
Wenn es Ihnen nicht ungelegen ist.
ven ess EE-nen nikht OON-gheh-leh-ghen isst.

Sorry I am late.
Es tut mir leid, daß ich spät komme.
ess toot meer lite, dahss ikh shpayt KO-meh.

The traffic was awful.
Der Verkehr war entsetzlich.
der fair-KAIR vahr ent-ZETS-likh.

Very happy to see you.
Sehr erfreut, Sie wiederzusehen.
zair air-FROYT, zee VEE-der-ts'oo-zay'en.

Make yourself at home!
Fühlen Sie sich wie zu Hause!
FŮ-len zee zikh vee ts'oo HOW-zeh!

---

1. Pronounce *ů* like "ee" with your lips in a tight circle.
2. *kh* is a guttural sound.
3. Stress the syllables in capital letters.

What a beautiful house!
Was für ein schönes Haus!
vahss für ine SHERN-ess howss!

Will you have something to drink?
Möchten Sie etwas zu trinken?
MERK-ten zee ET-vahss ts'oo TRINK'en?

A cigarette?	**To your health!**
Eine Zigarette?	Auf Ihr Wohl!
INE-eh ts'ig-ah-RET-teh?	*owf eer vohl!*

Dinner is served!
Das Abendessen ist serviert!
dahss AH-bent-ess-en isst sair-VEERT!

Will you sit here?
Wollen Sie hier sitzen?
VOHL-len zee heer ZITS'en?

What a delicious meal!	**It tastes great!**
Was für ein köstliches	Es schmeckt großartig!
Essen!	*ess shmekt GROSS-art-ikh!*
vahss für ine KERST-likh-	
ess ESS'en!	

Do have some more!
Nehmen Sie doch mehr!
NAY-men zee dokh mair!

We had a wonderful time!
Wir hatten viel Vergnügen!
veer HAHT'en feel fairg-NŮG-en!

We enjoyed visiting you.
Es war sehr nett bei Ihnen.
ess vahr zair nett by EEN-en.

I'm sorry, we must go.
Es tut mir leid, wir müssen gehen.
ess toot meer lite, veer MŮS-sen GAY'en.

We're taking an early plane.
Wir nehmen ein früheres Flugzeug.
veer NAY-men ein FRÜ-heh-ress FLOOK-ts'oig.

That is a pity!
Wie schade!
vee SHA-deh!

I'll take you to the hotel.
Ich bringe Sie zum Hotel.
ikh BRING-eh zee ts'oom ho-TEL.

No, please don't bother!
Nein, bitte bemühen Sie sich nicht!
nine, BIT-teh beh-MÜ'en zee sikh nikht!

Many thanks for your hospitality!
Vielen Dank für Ihre Gastfreundschaft!
FEEL-en dahnk für EER-eh GAHST-froynt-shahft!

You're welcome.
Bitte.
BIT-teh.

It was a pleasure for us.
Es war ein Vergnügen für uns.
Ess var ine fairg-NÜG-en für oonts.

Come back soon!
Kommen Sie bald wieder!
KOHM-men zee bahlt VEE-dehr!

Good-bye.
Auf Wiedersehen.
owf VEE-dehr-seh'n.

All the best!
Alles gute!
AH-less GOO-teh!

---

1. Pronounce *ů* like "ee" with your lips in a tight circle.
2. *kh* is a guttural sound.
3. Stress the syllables in capital letters.

14. Talking to People

Most phrase books are too preoccupied with attending to one's wants and generally "getting along" to pay much attention to what you should say once you have met someone. The following expressions have been tested for everyday conversational frequency and used and, except for the rather special phrases at the end of the section, will be of immediate use for making conversation with anyone you meet.

Do you live in this city?
Wohnen Sie in dieser Stadt?
VO-nen zee in DEE-zer shtaht?

Where are you from?
Wo kommen Sie her?
vo KOHM'en zee hair?

I am from Munich.
Ich komme aus München.
ikh KOHM-eh owss MÜNT-yen.

Really?
Wirklich?
VEERK-likh?

It's a beautiful city!
Es ist eine schöne Stadt!
ess isst INE-eh SHERN-eh shtaht!

I've been there.
Ich war dort.
ikh var dort.

I would like to go there.
Ich möchte dorthin fahren.
ikh MERKH-teh DORT-hin FAR'en.

How long have you been here?
Wie lange sind Sie schon hier?
vee LAHNG-eh zint zee shohn heer?

---

1. Pronounce *ü* like "ee" with your lips in a tight circle.
2. *kh* is a guttural sound.
3. Stress the syllables in capital letters.

Three days.
Drei Tage.
dry TAHG-eh.

Several weeks.
Einige Wochen.
EYE-nig-eh VOKH-en.

Two months.
Zwei Monate.
ts'vy MO-na-teh.

How long will you stay here?
Wie lange werden Sie hier bleiben?
vee LAHNG-eh VAIRD'en zee heer BLY-ben?

I will stay for one month.
Ich werde einen Monat bleiben.
ikh VAIRD-eh INE-en MO-naht BLY-ben.

Have you been here before?
Waren Sie schon früher hier?
VAR'en zee shohn FRÜ-er heer?

Yes, once.
Ja, einmal.
ya, INE-mahl.

Five years ago.
Vor fünf Jahren.
for fünf YA-ren.

A long time ago.
Vor langer Zeit.
for LAHNG-er ts'ite.

Before the war.
Vor dem Krieg.
for dem kreek.

Where are you living?
Wo wohnen Sie?
vo VOHN'en zee?

At what hotel?
In welchem Hotel?
in VEL-khem ho-TEL?

How do you like Vienna?
Wie gefällt Ihnen Wien?
vee ghe-FAILT EEN-en veen?

I like it very much.
Ich mag es sehr.
ikh mahk ess zair.

Very interesting.
Sehr interessant.
zair in-teh-reh-SAHNT.

The women are very beautiful.
Die Frauen sind sehr schön.
dee FROW-en zint zair shern.

Do you come from the United States?
Kommen Sie von den Vereinigten Staaten?
KOHM'en zee fohn den fair-EYE-nikh-ten SHTAHT-en?

Yes, from San Francisco.
Ja, von San Franzisko.
ya, fohn San Francisco.

I speak a little German
Ich spreche ein wenig Deutsch.
ikh SHPREKH-eh ine VEH-nikh doych.

Your pronunciation is good.
Ihre Aussprache ist gut.
EER-eh OWSS-shpra-kheh isst goot.

You are very kind.
Sie sind sehr liebenswürdig.
zee zint zair LEE-bens-vŭr-dikh.

Have you been in the United States?
Waren Sie schon in den Vereinigten Staaten?
VAR'en zee shohn in den fair-EYE-nikh-ten SHTAHT-en?

. . . In England?	**Where did you go?**
. . . in England?	Wo waren Sie?
. . . in EHNG-lahnt?	*vo VAR'en zee?*

What do you think of . . . ?
Was halten Sie von . . . ?
vahss HAHLT'en zee fohn . . . ?

---

1. Pronounce *ŭ* like "ee" with your lips in a tight circle.
2. *kh* is a guttural sound.
3. Stress the syllables in capital letters.

. . . American movies?
. . . amerikanischen Filmen?
. . . ah-meh-ree-KA-nee-shen FILM-en?

. . . German music?
. . . deutscher Musik?
. . . DOY-cher moo-ZEEK?

. . . German books?
. . . deutschen Büchern?
. . . DOY-chen BÜ-khern?

When people ask your opinion about something, you will
find the following comments most helpful.

Very interesting.
Sehr interessant.
zair in-teh-reh-SAHNT.

Great!	**Magnificent!**
Großartig!	Prachtvoll!
GROSS-art-ikh!	*PRAKHT-fohl!*
Marvelous!	**Not bad.**
Wunderbar!	Nicht schlecht.
VOON-der-bar!	*nikht shlekht.*
Sometimes.	**Once.**
Manchmal.	Einst.
MAHNKH-mahl.	*ine'st.*
Never.	**Often.**
Niemals.	Oft.
NEE-mahlss.	*ohft.*

It seems to me that . . .
Es scheint mir, daß . . .
ess shine't meer, dahss . . .

In any case . . .
Auf jeden Fall . . .
owf YEH-den fahl . . .

Really?
Wirklich?
VEERK-likh?

That's too bad!
Das ist schade!
dahss isst SHA-deh!

I don't know.
Ich weiß nicht.
ikh vice nikht.

I have forgotten.
Ich habe vergessen.
ikh HAHB-eh fair-GUESS'en.

I agree with you.
Ich bin Ihrer Meinung.
ikh bin EER-er MY-noong.

Of course.
Selbstverständlich.
zelpst-fair-SHTEND-likh.

Is it possible?
Ist es möglich?
isst ess MERG-likh?

Unbelievable!
Unglaublich!
oon-GL'OWB-likh!

You must come to see us soon.
Sie müsen uns bald besuchen.
zee MÜSS'en oons bahlt beh-ZOOKH'en.

At our house.
Bei uns zu Hause.
by oons ts'oo HOW-zeh.

With pleasure.
Mit Vergnügen.
mit fairg-NÜG-en.

Are you married?
Sind Sie verheiratet?
zint zee fair-HI-raht-et?

I am married.
Ich bin verheiratet.
ikh bin fair-HI-raht-et.

I am not married.
Ich bin nicht verheiratet.
ikh bin nikht fair-HI-raht-et.

---

1. Pronounce *ů* like "ee" with your lips in a tight circle.
2. *kh* is a guttural sound.
3. Stress the syllables in capital letters.

Do you have children?
Haben Sie Kinder?
HAHB'en zee KIN-der?

No, I haven't.
Nein, ich habe keine.
nine, ikh HAHB-eh KYE-neh.

Yes, I have children.
Ja, ich habe Kinder.
yah, ikh HAHB-eh KIN-der.

How many girls?
Wieviel Mädchen?
VEE-feel MAID-khen?

How many boys?
Wieviel Jungen?
VEE-feel YOONG'en?

How old are they?
Wie alt sind sie?
vee ahlt zint zee?

My son is seven years old.
Mein Sohn ist sieben Jahre alt.
mine zohn isst ZEE-ben YA-reh ahlt.

My daughter is ten years old.
Meine Tochter ist zehn Jahre alt.
My-neh TOKH-ter isst ts'ayn YA-reh ahlt.

What cute children!
Was für süße Kinder!
vahss für ZÜ-seh KIN-der!

This is my . . .
Das ist meine . . .
dahss isst MY-neh . . .

. . . mother.
. . . Mutter.
. . . MOOT-er.

. . . wife.
. . . Frau.
. . . frow.

. . . sister.
. . . Schwester.
. . . SHVESS-ter.

. . . daughter.
. . . Tochter.
. . . TOKH-ter.

. . . daughter-in-law.
. . . Schwiegertochter.
. . . SHVEE-gher-tokh-ter.

. . . granddaughter.
. . . Enkelin.
. . . EN-kel-in.

This is my . . .
Das ist mein . . .
dahss isst mine . . .

. . . father.
. . . Vater.
. . . FA-ter.

. . . husband.
. . . Mann.
. . . mahn.

... brother.　　... son.　　　　　... grandson.
... Bruder.　　... Sohn.　　　　... Enkel.
... *BROOD-er.*　... *zohn.*　　　... *ENK-el.*

... son-in-law.　　　　　... **Do you know**
... Schwiegersohn.　　　... Kennen Sie
... *SHVEE-gher-zohn.*　　... *KEN-nen zee*

... Mr. Peters?　　　　... that man?
... Herrn Peters?　　　... diesen Mann?
... *Hairn PAY-terss?*　... *DEE-zen mahn?*

... Mrs. Muller?　　　　... that lady?
... Frau Müller?　　　　... diese Dame?
... *frow MÜL-er?*　　　... *DEE-zeh DA-meh?*

He is ...　　　　　　... a writer.
Er ist ...　　　　　... Schriftsteller.
air isst ...　　　　... *SHRIFT-shtel-ler.*

... an artist.　　　　... a businessman.
... Künstler.　　　　... Geschäftsmann.
... *KÜNST-ler.*　　　... *gheh-SHEFTS-mahn.*

... a lawyer.　　　　... a doctor.
... Rechtsanwalt.　　... Arzt.
... *REKHTS-ahn-vahlt.*　... *arts't.*

... a manufacturer.　　... a painter.
... Fabrikant.　　　　... Maler.
... *fa-bree-KAHNT.*　　... *MA-ler.*

... a banker.　　　　... a professor.
... Bankier.　　　　... Professor.
... *bahnk-YEH.*　　　... *pro-FESS-or.*

---

1. Pronounce *ů* like "ee" with your lips in a tight circle.
2. *kh* is a guttural sound.
3. Stress the syllables in capital letters.

. . . an actor.
. . . Schauspieler
. . . *SH'OW-shpeel-er.*

. . . a member of the
government.
. . . Regierungsmitglied.
. . *reh-GEER-oongs-
mit-gleet.*

. . . a scientist.
. . . Wissenschaftler.
. . . *VISS-en-shahft-ler.*

. . . an engineer.
. . . Ingenieur.
. . . *en-zhen-ERR.*

. . . a soldier.
. . . Soldat
. . . *zohl-DAHT.*

. . . an officer.
. . . Offizier.
. . . *oh-fee-TS'EER.*

She is . . .
Sie ist . . .
zee isst . . .

. . . an actress.
. . . Schauspielerin.
. . . *SH'OW-shpeel-er-in.*

. . . an airline hostess.
. . . Stewardesse.
. . . *STEW-ar-dess-eh.*

. . . teacher. (f)
. . . Lehrerin.
. . . *LAIR-er-in.*

. . . a writer. (f)
. . . Schriftstellerin.
. . . *SHRIFT-shtel-ler-in.*

. . . a doctor. (f)
. . . Ärztin.
. . . *AIRTS-tin.*

. . . an artist. (f)
. . . Künstlerin.
. . . *KÜNST-ler-in.*

. . . my wife.
. . . meine Frau.
. . . *MY-neh frow.*

He is an American.
Er ist Amerikaner.
*air isst ah-meh-ree-
KAHN-er.*

She is an American.
Sie ist Amerikanerin.
*zee isst ah-meh-ree-
KAHN-er-in.*

He is a German.
Er ist Deutscher.
air isst DOYCH-er.

She is a German.
Sie ist Deutsche.
zee isst DOYCH-eh.

He is an Austrian.
Er ist Österreicher.
air isst ER-stair-RYE-kher.

She is an Austrian.
Sie ist Österreicherin.
zee isst ER-stair-RYE-kher-in.

He is a Swiss.
Er ist Schweizer.
air isst SHVITE-ser.

She is a Swiss.
Sie ist Schweizerin.
zee isst SHVITE-ser-in.

He is an Englishman.
Er ist Engländer.
air isst EHNG-len-der.

She is an Englishwoman.
Sie ist Engländerin.
zee isst EHNG-len-der-in.

He is a Canadian.
Er ist Kanadier.
air isst ka-NAHD-yer.

She is a Canadian.
Sie ist Kanadierin.
zee isst ka-NAHD-yer-in.

See dictionary for other selected nationalities.

He (she) is very intelligent.
Er (Sie) ist sehr intelligent.
air (zee) isst zair in-tel-lee-GHENT.

He (she) is very nice.
Er (Sie) ist sehr nett.
air (zee) isst zair net.

He (she) is very capable.
Er (Sie) ist sehr tüchtig.
air (zee) isst zair tǔkh-tikh.

This is my address.
Das ist meine Adresse.
dahss isst MINE-eh ah-DRESS-eh.

---

1. Pronounce *ǔ* like "ee" with your lips in a tight circle.
2. *kh* is a guttural sound.
3. Stress the syllables in capital letters.

What is your (his, her) address?
Was ist Ihre (seine, ihre) Adresse?
vahss isst EER-eh (ZY-neh, EER-eh) ah-DRESS-eh?

Here is my telephone number.
Hier ist meine Telefonnummer.
heer isst MINE-eh teh-leh-FOHN-noom-er.

What is your telephone number?
Wie ist Ihre Telefonnummer?
vee isst EER-eh teh-leh-FOHN-noom-er?

May I call you?
Darf ich Sie anrufen?
darf ikh zee AHN-roof'en?

When?
Wann?
vahn?

Tomorrow morning.
Morgen Vormittag.
Mor-ghen FOR-mit-tahk.

Early
Früh.
frü.

In the afternoon.
Am Nachmittag.
ahm NAKH-mit-tahk.

What is your first name?
Wie ist Ihr Vorname?
vee isst eer FOR-na-meh?

My first name is Peter.
Mein Vorname ist Peter.
mine FOR-na-meh isst PAY-ter.

You dance very well.
Sie tanzen sehr gut.
zee TAHN-ts'en zair goot.

You sing very well.
Sie singen sehr gut.
zee ZING'en zair goot.

I like your dress.
Mir gefällt Ihr Kleid.
meer gheh-FELT eer klite.

I have a surprise for you.
Ich habe eine Überraschung für Sie.
ikh HAHB-eh INE-eh über-RAHSH-oong für zee.

Do you like it?
Gefällt es Ihnen?
gheh-FELT ess EEN-en?

May I see you again?
Darf ich Sie wiedersehen?
darf ikh zee VEE-der-zay'en?

When?
Wann?
vahn?

Where?
Wo?
vo?

What's the matter?
Was ist los?
vahss isst lohss?

Are you angry?
Sind Sie böse?
zint zee BER-zeh?

Why?
Warum?
va-ROOM?

I'm very sorry.
Es tut mir sehr leid.
ess toot meer zehr lite.

Where are you going?
Wo gehen Sie hin?
vo GAY'en zee hin?

Let's go together!
Gehen wir zusammen!
GAY'en veer ts'oo-ZAHM-en!

You are very clever.
Sie sind sehr klug.
zee zint zair klook.

You are very pretty . . .
Sie sind sehr hübsch . . .
zee zint zair hübsch . . .

and very charming too.
und auch sehr sympathisch.
*oont owkh zair
      seem-PA-tish.*

---

1. Pronounce *ü* like "ee" with your lips in a tight circle.
2. *kh* is a guttural sound.
3. Stress the syllables in capital letters.

You are very nice.
Sie sind sehr nett.
zee zint zair net.

I like you very much.
Ich mag Sie sehr gern.
ikh mahk zee zair gairn.

What do you think of me?
Was halten Sie von mir?
vahss HAHLT'en zee fohn meer?

I love you.
Ich liebe dich.
ikh LEEB-eh dikh.

Are you serious?
Meinst du es ernst?
MINE'st doo ess airnst?

Will you give me your photograph?
Wirst du mir dein Foto geben?
veerst doo meer dine FO-toh GAY-ben?

Will you write to me?
Wirst du mir schreiben?
veerst doo meer SHRY-ben?

Don't forget!
Nicht vergessen!
nikht fair-GUESS'en!

In the last five sentences we have used the familiar form for "you," both in the verb and the pronoun (**du**), since the tone of the conversation implies a certain degree of familiarity. See the introduction to the "Dictionary" for more about the familiar form.

15. Words That Show You Are "With It"

There are certain words that German-speaking people use constantly but that do not always have an exact equivalent in English. To use them at the right time will cause German people to consider that you have good manners and are familiar with the most frequent German conversational phrases—in other words, that you are "with it." The German expressions are given first to make it easier for you to recognize them as they occur in everyday conversation.

We have divided these terms into two groups. The first is composed of selected polite expressions:

Verzeihung!
fair-TS'Y-oong!
Pardon me!

Gute Reise!
GOOT-eh RYE-zeh!
Have a good trip!

Herzlich willkommen!
HAIRTS-likh vil-KOHM-en!
A hearty welcome!

Prosit!
PRO-zit!
Here's to you!

Guten Appetit!
GOOT-en ahp-peh-TEET!
Enjoy your meal!

Auf Ihre Gesundheit!
owf EER-eh gheh-ZOONT-hite!
To your good health!

Mahlzeit!
MAHL-ts'ite!
Mealtime! (often said when sitting down at or leaving the table)

---

1. Pronounce *ů* like "ee" with your lips in a tight circle.
2. *kh* is a guttural sound.
3. Stress the syllables in capital letters.

Alles Gute!
AH-less GOOT-eh!
All the best! (or) Have a
  good time!

Viel Glück!
feel glŭk!
Good luck!

Hals und Beinbruch!
hahlss oont BINE-brookh!
Good luck! (literally "Neck and leg break!")

Herzliche Glückwünsche!
*HAIRTS-likh-eh
  GLUK-vŭn-sheh!*
Congratulations!

Mein Beileid!
mine BY-lite!
My sympathy!

Mit besten Grüßen!
mit BESS-ten GRŬ-sen!
With best regards!

Gute Besserung!
GOOT-eh BESS-eh-roong!
Get well!

Viele Grüsse an _____ !
FEEL-eh GRŬSS-eh ahn _____ !
My regards to _____ !

As the following phrases permeate conversation, it will
interest you to know what they mean, as well as to learn to
use them as useful conversational stopgaps. The translations
are extremely free, as these expressions are very idiomatic.

Nicht wahr?
nikht var?
Isn't it? (or) Don't you
  think so?

Doch
dohkh
then (or) however

Jawohl!
ya-VOHL!
Yes, indeed!

Es tut mir leid!
ess toot meer lite!
I'm sorry!

Dann
dahnn
then

Wie, bitte?
vee, BIT-teh?
How's that?

Bitte sehr.
BIT-teh zair.
Please (or) You're welcome.

Gehen wir!
GAY'en veer!
Let's go!

Das ist schrecklich!
dahss isst SHREK-likh!
That's terrible!

Das macht nichts.
dahss makht nikhts.
It doesn't matter.

Das ist mir egal.
dahss isst meer eh-GAHL.
I don't care.

Prima!
PREE-ma!
The best!

Großartig!
GROSS-art-ikh!
Wonderful!

Einverstanden!
INE-fer-shtahnd'en!
Okay.

Abgemacht!
AHP-gheh-mahkht!
It's a deal!

Natürlich.
na-TǓR-likh.
Naturally.

Irgendwo.
EER-ghent-vo.
Somewhere.

Irgendwie.
EER-ghent-vee.
Somehow.

Selbstverständlich.
zelbst-fair-SHTEND-likh.
Of course.

Aber nein!
AH-bair nine!
But no!

Aber ja!
AH-bair ya!
But yes!

Ebenfalls!
AIB-en-fahlss!
Mutually (or)
        Same to you!

Bestimmt.
beh-SHTIMMT.
Definitely.

Wirklich?
VEERK-likh?
Really?

Tatsächlich.
taht-ZEKH-likh.
Indeed.

Sofort!
zo-FORT!
Right away!

---

1. Pronounce ǔ like "ee" with your lips in a tight circle.
2. *kh* is a guttural sound.
3. Stress the syllables in capital letters.

Hören Sie mal!
her'en zee mahl!
Listen! (or) Look here!

Was Sie nicht sagen!
vahss zee nikht ZA-ghen!
You don't say!

Gar nicht.
gar nikht.
Not at all

Übrigens.
Ü-bree-ghenss.
Incidentally.

Um Gottes Willen!
oom GOHT-ess VILL-en!
For God's sake! (or) For Heaven's sake!

Das ist unglaublich!
dahss isst oon-GL'OWB-likh!
That's incredible!

Mein Gott!
mine goht!
My God (or) Good heavens!

Gott sei Dank!
goht zye dahnk!
Thank God! (or) Thank goodness!

16. Shopping

Shops in Germany, Austria, and Switzerland still tend to be specialized, although there exist chains of general stores and even the supermarket—**Supermarkt.**

Some additional shop signs you will see include **Delikatessen,** which should need no translation but means a specialty food shop, and **Drogerie,** which does not exactly correspond to "drugstore" as it sells only soap, perfumes, and cosmetics. **Boutique** is frequently used for small shops. On some cafés or small shops **bei** (at the house of) precedes a proper name. **Bei Giesele** means "at Giesele's house" or "at Giesele's."

Names of Shops

Is there a . . . around here?
Gibt es in der Nähe . . .
ghipt ess in dair NAY-eh . . .

. . . a department store?
. . . ein Warenhaus?
. . . ine VAR-en-howss?

. . . a dress shop?
. . . ein Kleidergeschäft?
. . . ine KLY-der gheh-sheft?

. . . a hat shop?
. . . ein Hutgeschäft?
. . . ine HOOT-gheh-sheft?

. . . a shoe store?
. . . ein Schuhgeschäft?
. . . ine SHOO-gheh-sheft?

. . . a jewelry shop?
. . . ein Juweliergeschäft?
. . . ine yoo-veh-LEER-gheh-sheft?

. . . a drugstore? (for soap, cosmetics, perfumes, etc.)
. . . eine Drogerie?
. . . INE-eh dro-gheh-REE?

---

1. Pronounce *ů* like "ee" with your lips in a tight circle.
2. *kh* is a guttural sound.
3. Stress the syllables in capital letters.

. . . a pharmacy? (for medicines)
. . . eine Apotheke?
. . . *INE-eh ah-po-TEH-keh?*

. . . a bookshop?
. . . eine Buchhandlung?
. . . *INE-eh BOOKH-hahnt-loong?*

. . . a toy shop?
. . . ein Spielzeuggeschäft?
. . . *ine SHPEEL-ts'oyk-gheh-sheft?*

. . . a flower shop?
. . . einen Blumenladen?
. . . *INE-en BLOOM-en-la-den?*

. . . an antique shop?
. . . ein Antiquitätengeschäft?
. . . *ine ahn-tee-kvee-TAYT-en-gheh-sheft?*

. . . a grocery store?
. . . einen Kolonialwarenladen?
. . . *INE-en ko-lohn-YAHL-va-ren-la-den?*

. . . a market?
. . . einen Markt?
. . . *INE-en markt?*

. . . a camera shop?
. . . ein Fotogeschäft?
. . . *ine FO-toh-gheh-sheft?*

. . . a tobacco shop?
. . . einen Tabakladen?
. . . *INE-en ta-BAHK-la-den?*

. . . a barbershop?
. . . einen Friseur?
. . . *INE-en free-ZERR?*

. . . a beauty parlor?
. . . einen Damenfriseur?
. . . *INE-en DA-men-free-ZERR?*

General Shopping Vocabulary

BARGAIN SALE
AUSVERKAUF
OWSS-fer kowf

ON SALE
ZUM VERKAUF
ts'oom fair-KOWF

May I help you?
Darf ich Ihnen helfen?
darf ikh EEN-en HELL-fen?

What do you wish?
Was wünschen Sie?
vahss VÜN-shen zee?

I would like something . . .
Ich möchte etwas . . .
ikh MERKH-teh ET-vahss . . .

. . . for my husband.
. . . für meinen Mann.
. . . für MY-nen mahn.

. . . for my wife.
. . . für meine Frau.
. . . für MY-neh frow.

. . . for a man.
. . . für einen Herren.
. . . für INE-en hairn.

. . . for a lady.
. . . für eine Dame.
. . . für INE-eh DA-meh.

Do you need something?
Brauchen Sie etwas?
BROW-khen zee ET-vahss?

At the moment—nothing.
Momentan—nichts.
mo-men-TAHN-nikhts.

I'm just looking around.
Ich sehe mir bloß alles an.
ikh ZAY-eh meer blohss AH-less ahn.

I'll be back later.
Ich komme später wieder.
ikh KOHM-eh SHPAY-ter VEE-der.

---

1. Pronounce *ü* like "ee" with your lips in a tight circle.
2. *kh* is a guttural sound.
3. Stress the syllables in capital letters.

I like this.   **. . . that.**   **How much is it?**
Ich mag dies.   . . . das.   Wieviel macht es?
ikh mahk deess.   *. . . dahss.*   *vee-FEEL makht ess?*

Show me another.
Zeigen Sie mir ein anderes.
TS'Y-ghen zee meer ine AHN-der-ess.

Something not so expensive.   **Do you like this?**
Etwas nicht so teuer.   Gefällt das Ihnen?
ET-vahss nikht zo TOY-er.   *gheh-FELT dahss EEN-en?*

May I try it on?
Darf ich es anprobieren?
darf ikh ess AHN-pro-beer'en?

That suits you marvelously!
Das paßt Ihnen wunderbar!
dahss pahst EEN-en VOON-der-bar!

Good, I'll take it.
Gut, ich nehme es.
goot, ikh NEH-meh ess.

Can you alter it?
Können Sie es umändern?
KERN-en zee ess OOM-end-ern?

Is it handmade?   **Is it hand-embroidered?**
Ist es Handarbeit?   Ist es handgestickt?
isst ess HAHNT-ar-bite?   *isst ess HAHNT-gheh-*
                                 shtikt?

Would you wrap it?
Würden Sie es einpacken?
VÛR-den zee ess INE-pahk'en?

Can I pay by check?
Kann ich mit einem Scheck zahlen?
kahn ikh mit INE-em shek TS'AHL'en?

Can you send it to this address?
Können Sie es an diese Adresse senden?
KERN'en zee ess ahn DEE-zeh ah-DRESS-eh ZEND'en?

A receipt, please.
Eine Quittung, bitte.
INE-eh KVIT-toong, BIT-teh.

The change, please.
Das Wechselgeld, bitte.
dahss VEX-el-ghelt,
   BIT-teh.

And some small change.
Und etwas Kleingeld.
oont ET-vahss
   KLINE-ghelt.

Come back again!
Kommen Sie bald wieder!
KOHM'en zee bahlt VEE-der!

POINT TO THE ANSWER

To make certain you and the salesperson understand the details, you may wish to use this "Point to the Answer" section.

The sentence in German after the arrow asks the salesperson to point to the answer.

 Zeigen Sie bitte hierunter Ihr Antwort auf meine Frage. Vielen Dank.

Wir haben keines.
We haven't any.

Das ist alles, was wir haben.
That's all we have.

---

1. Pronounce *ü* like "ee" with your lips in a tight circle.
2. *kh* is a guttural sound.
3. Stress the syllables in capital letters.

Wir haben nichts größeres.	**Wir haben nichts kleineres.**
We haven't anything larger.	We haven't anything smaller.

Wir liefern nicht.	**Wir nehmen Reiseschecks.**
We don't deliver.	We accept traveler's checks.

Wir können es an eine Adresse in Amerika senden.
We can send it to an address in America.

Was ist Ihre Adresse?
What is your address?

Wir können nicht persönliche Schecks nehmen.
We cannot accept personal checks.

Clothes

a blouse	a suit	a coat
eine Bluse	ein Anzug	ein Mantel
INE-eh BLOO-zeh	*ine AHN-ts'ook*	*ine MAHN-tel*

a hat	a scarf	a handbag
ein Hut	ein Schal	eine Handtasche
ine hoot	*ine shahl*	*INE-eh HAHNT-ta-sheh*

gloves	shoes	stockings
Handschuhe	Schuhe	Strümpfe
HAHNT-shoo-eh	*SHOO-eh*	*STRÜMPF-eh*

a slip	a brassiere
ein Unterrock	ein Büstenhalter
ine OONT-er-rohk	*ine BÜ-sten-hahl-ter*

panties	a nightgown
Schlüpfer	ein Nachthemd
SHLÜP-fer	*ine NAKHT-hemt*

a bathrobe
ein Bademantel
ine BA-deh-mahn-tel

slippers
Pantoffeln
pahn-TOHF-feln

an evening dress
ein Abendkleid
ine AH-bent-klite

a raincoat
ein Regenmantel
ine REH-ghen-mahn-tel.

boots
Stiefel
SHTEE-fel

an umbrella
ein Regenschirm
ine REH-ghen-sheerm

a swimsuit
ein Badeanzug
ine BA-deh-ahn-ts'ook

sandals
Sandalen
zahn-DAHL-en

a skirt
ein Rock
ine rohk

pants
Hosen
HO-zen

a jacket
eine Jacke
INE-eh YA-keh

a tie
eine Krawatte
INE-eh kra-VAHT-teh

socks
Socken
ZOHK-en

an overcoat
ein Mantel
ine MAHN-tel

undershorts
Unterhosen
OONT-er-ho-zen

an undershirt
ein Unterhemd
ine OONT-er-hemt

pajamas
Pyjama
pee-JAHM-ah

handkerchiefs
Taschentücher
TAHSH-en-tŭkh-er

---

1. Pronounce *ŭ* like "ee" with your lips in a tight circle.
2. *kh* is a guttural sound.
3. Stress the syllables in capital letters.

Sizes—Colors—Materials

What size?
Welche Größe?
VELL-kheh GRER-seh?

small	medium	large	larger
klein	mittel	groß	größer
kline	*MIT-el*	*gross*	*GRER-ser*

smaller	wider	narrower	longer
kleiner	weiter	enger	länger
KLINE-er	*VITE-er*	*EHNG-er*	*LENG-er*

shorter	**What color?**
kürzer	Welche Farbe?
KÜR-ts'er	*VEL-kheh FAR-beh?*

blue	red	yellow	green	lilac
blau	rot	gelb	grün	lila
bl'ow	*roht*	*ghelp*	*grün*	*LEE-la*

brown	gray	black	white
braun	grau	schwarz	weiß
brown	*gr'ow*	*shvarts*	*vice*

darker	lighter
dunkler	heller
DOONK-ler	*HELL-er*

Is it silk?	**wool**	**linen**
Ist es Seide?	Wolle	Leinen
isst ess ZY-deh?	*VOHL-leh*	*LYE-nen*

nylon	dacron	leather	suede
Nylon	Dacron	Leder	Wildleder
NEE-lohn	*DAHK-rohn*	*LAY-der*	*VILD-lay-der*

kid
Ziegenleder
*TS'EE-ghen-lay-
der*

cotton
Baumwolle
B'OWM-vohl-leh

plastic
Kunststoff
KOONST-stohff

fur
Pelz
pelts

What kind of fur?
Was für ein Pelz?
vahss für ine pelts?

fox
Fuchs
fooks

beaver
Biber
BEE-ber

seal
Seehund
ZAY-hoont

mink
Nerz
nairts

leopard
Leopard
leh'o-PART

rabbit
Kaninchen
kah-NEEN-khen

Newsstand

I would like . . .
Ich möchte . . .
ikh MERKH-teh . . .

a guidebook
einen Reiseführer
INE-en RYE-zeh-für-er

a map of the city
einen Stadtplan
INE-en STAHT-plahn

sunglasses
eine Sonnenbrille
INE-eh ZOHN-nen-bril-eh

postcards
Postkarten
POST-kar-ten

some paper
etwas Papier
ET-vahss pa-PEER

this magazine
diese Zeitschrift
DEE-zeh TS'ITE-shrift

an American newspaper
eine amerikanische Zeitung
INE-eh ah-meh-ree-KA-nee-sheh TS'ITE-oong

---

1. Pronounce *ü* like "ee" with your lips in a tight circle.
2. *kh* is a guttural sound.
3. Stress the syllables in capital letters.

Tobacco Shop

Have you American cigarettes?
Haben Sie amerikanische Zigaretten?
HAHB'en zee ah-meh-ree-KA-nee-sheh ts'ee-ga-RET-en?

a pipe	**tobacco**	**cigars**
eine Pfeife	Tabak	Zigarren
INE-eh PFY-feh	*ta-BAHK*	*ts'ee-GA-ren*

matches	**a lighter**	**lighter fluid**
Streichhölzer	ein Feuerzeug	Benzin
SHTRY'KH-herl-ts'er	*ine FOY-er-ts'oyk*	*ben-TS'EEN*

Drugstore

a toothbrush	**toothpaste**
eine Zahnbürste	Zahnpasta
INE-eh TS'AHN-bůr-steh	*TS'AHN-pa-sta*

a razor	**razor blades**
ein Rasierapparat	Rasierklingen
ine ra-ZEER-ah-par-raht	*ra-ZEER-kling-en*

shaving cream	**a hairbrush**
Rasiercreme	eine Haarbürste
ra-ZEER-krehm	*INE-eh HAR-bůr-steh*

a comb	**aspirin**
ein Kamm	Aspirin
ine kahm	*ah-spear-EEN*

iodine	**scissors**
Jod	eine Schere
yoht	*INE-eh SHAIR-eh*

a nail file
eine Nagelfeile
INE-eh NA-ghel-fy-leh

antiseptic
antiseptisches Mittel
ahn-tee-SEP-tish-es MIT-el

cough medicine
Hustensaft
HOOSS-ten-zahft

cough drops
Hustenbonbons
HOOSS-ten-bohn-bohnss

Cosmetics

powder
Puder
POO-der

lipstick
Lippenstift
LIP-pen-shtift

nail polish
Nagellack
NA-ghel-lahk

mascara
Wimperntusche
VIM-pern-too-sheh

cleansing cream
Reinigungscreme
RYE-nee-goongs-kreh-meh

shampoo
Schampo
shahm-POO

eyebrow pencil
Augenbraustift
OW-ghen-brow-shtift

bobby pins
Haarklammern
HAR-klahm-ern

hairpins
Haarnadeln
HAR-nahd-eln

hairspray
Haarlack
HAR-lahk

perfume
Parfüm
par-FÜM

That smells good, doesn't it?
Das riecht gut, nicht wahr?
dahss reekht goot, nikht var?

---

1. Pronounce *ü* like "ee" with your lips in a tight circle.
2. *kh* is a guttural sound.
3. Stress the syllables in capital letters.

Hairdresser

Wash and set, please.
Waschen und Legen, bitte.
VA-shen oont LAY-ghen, BIT-teh.

Tint it, please.
Tönen, bitte
TER-nen, BIT-teh.

lighter
heller
HELL-er

darker
dunkler
DOONK-ler

a manicure
eine Maniküre
INE-eh ma-nee-KŮ-reh

a pedicure
eine Pediküre
INE-eh ped-ee-KŮ-reh

Barber

a shave
rasieren
ra-ZEE'ren

a haircut
ein Haarschnitt
ine HAR-shnit

a massage
eine Massage
INE-eh ma-SA-zheh

Use scissors!
Mit der Schere!
mitt dair SHEH-reh!

shorter
kürzer
KŮR-ts'er

not too short
nicht zu kurz
nikht ts'oo koorts

on top
oben
OH-ben

in back
hinten
HIN-ten

the sides
die Seiten
dee ZY-ten

That's fine!
Das ist gut!
dahss isst goot!

Food Market

I would like . . .
Ich Möchte . . .
ihk MERKH-teh . . .

. . . a dozen . . .
. . . ein Dutzend . . .
. . . ine DOOTS-ent . . .

. . . of these.   . . . of those.
. . . von diesen.   . . . von denen.
. . . *fohn DEE-zen.*   . . . *fohn DEH-nen.*

I want five.   **Is this fresh?**
Ich möchte fünf.   Ist das frisch?
ikh MERKH-teh fůnf.   *isst dahss frish?*

Three cans of these preserves.
Drei Büchsen dieser Konserven.
dry BŮKH-zen DEE-zer kohn-ZAIR-ven.

How much per kilo?
Wieviel das Kilo?
vee-FEEL dahss KEE-lo?

   Weight is measured by the kilo (kilogram—**kilogramm**)
rather than by the pound. One kilo is equivalent to 2.2
pounds.

Do you have wine here?   **What is this?**
Gibt es Wein hier?   Was ist das?
ghipt ess vine heer?   *vahss isst dahss?*

strong liquor   **In a bag, please!**
Schnaps   In eine Tüte, bitte!
shnahps   *in INE-eh TŮ-teh, BIT-teh!*

Jewelry

I would like . . .
Ich möchte . . .
ikh MERKH-teh . . .

---

1. Pronounce *ů* like "ee" with your lips in a tight circle.
2. *kh* is a guttural sound.
3. Stress the syllables in capital letters.

a watch	a ring	a bracelet
eine Uhr	einen Ring	ein Armband
INE-eh oor	*INE-en ring*	*ine ARM-bahnt*

a necklace	earrings
ein Halsband	Ohrringe
ine HAHLSS-bahnt	*OHR-ring-eh*

Is it gold?	silver	platinum
Ist es aus Gold?	Silber	Platin
isst ess owss gohlt?	*ZIL-ber*	*pla-TEEN*

Is it silver-plated?	Is it gold-plated?
Ist es versilbert?	Ist es vergoldet?
isst ess fair-ZEEL-bairt?	*isst ess fair-GOHL-det?*

a diamond	a ruby
ein Diamant	ein Rubin
ine dee-ah-MAHNT	*ine ROO-bin*

pearls	a sapphire
Perlen	ein Saphir
PAIR-len	*ine zah-FEER*

Antiques

What period is this?
Aus welcher Zeit stammt dies?
owss VEL-kher ts'ite shtahmt deess?

It's beautiful!	But very expensive.
Es ist schön!	Aber sehr teuer.
ess isst shern!	*AH-ber zair TOY-er.*

How much is . . .	. . . this book?
Was kostet . . .	. . . dieses Buch?
vahss KO-stet . . .	*. . . DEE-zes bookh?*

. . . this picture?
. . . dieses Bild?
. . . *DEE-zess BILT?*

. . . this frame?
. . . dieser Rahmen?
. . . *DEE-zer RA-men?*

. . . this map?
. . . diese Landkarte?
. . . *DEE-zeh LAHNT-kar-teh?*

. . . this piece of furniture?
. . . dieses Möbelstück?
. . . *DEE-zess MER-bel-shtůk?*

Can you have it sent?
Können Sie es schicken lassen?
KERN'en zee ess SHICK'en LAHSS'en?

. . . to this address?
. . . an diese Adresse?
. . . *ahn DEE-zeh ah-DRESS-eh?*

---

1. Pronounce *ů* like "ee" with your lips in a tight circle.
2. *kh* is a guttural sound.
3. Stress the syllables in capital letters.

17. Telephone

Talking on the phone is an excellent test of your ability to communicate in German because you can't see the person you are talking to, nor use gestures to get your meaning across. When asking for someone, simply say his name and add **bitte**. If you say the number instead of dialing, say the numbers in pairs: 79–65–83 would be **neunundsiebzig–fünf-undsechzig–dreiundachtzig.**

Where is the telephone?
Wo ist das Telefon?
vo isst dahss teh-leh-FOHN?

The telephone operator.	**Hello.**
Das Telefonfräulein.	Hallo.
dahss teh-leh-FOHN-froy-line.	*HA-lo.*

Please, the telephone number of _____ .
Bitte, die Telefonnummer von _____ .
BIT-teh, dee teh-leh-FOHN-noom-er fohn _____ .

Connect me, please, with number _____ in Berlin.
Verbinden Sie mich, bitte, mit der Nummer _____ in Berlin.
fair-BIN-den zee mikh, BIT-teh, mit dair NOOM-er _____ in bair-LEEN.

Information.	**Long distance.**
Auskunft.	Ferngespräch.
OWSS-koonft.	*fairn-gheh-SHPREKH.*

I am calling number _____ , extension 339.
Ich rufe Nummer _____ , Apparat drei-drei-neun.
ikh ROO-feh NOOM-er _____ , ahp-pa-RAHT dry-dry-noyn.

---

1. Pronounce ü like "ee" with your lips in a tight circle.
2. *kh* is a guttural sound.
3. Stress the syllables in capital letters.

How long must I wait?
Wie lange muß ich warten?
vee LAHNG-eh mooss ikh VART'en?

How much is it per minute?
Wieviel kostet es pro Minute?
vee-FEEL KO-stet ess pro mee-NOO-teh?

My number is _____ .
Meine Nummer ist _____ .
MINE-eh NOOM-er isst _____ .

Mr. Schmidt, please.
Herrn Schmidt, bitte.
hairn shmit, BIT-teh.

He (she) isn't here.
Er (Sie) ist nicht da.
air (zee) isst nikht da.

Please say it once more.
Bitte sagen Sie es noch
einmal.
*BIT-teh ZAHG'en zee ess
nokh ine-MAHL.*

Hold the line!
Bleiben Sie am Apparat!
*BLYB'en zee ahm
ahp-pa-RAHT!*

One moment!
Einen Augenblick!
INE-en OW-ghen-blik!

When is he (she) coming back?
Wann kommt er (sie) zurück?
vahn kohmt air (zee) ts'oo-RŬK?

Thank you, I'll call back.
Danke schön, ich rufe wieder an.
DAHN-keh shern, ikh ROOF-eh VEE-der ahn.

Can you give him (her) the following message?
Können Sie ihm (ihr) das Folgende mitteilen?
*KERN'en zee eem (eer) dahss FOHL-ghen-deh
MIT-tile'en?*

Please ask him (her) to call me.
Bitten Sie ihn (sie) mich anzurufen.
BIT'en zee een (zee) mikh AHN-ts'oo-roof'en.

I'll give you my number.
Ich gebe Ihnen meine Nummer.
ikh GAY-beh EEN-en MINE-eh NOOM-er.

This is Brown speaking.
Hier spricht Brown.
heer shprikt brown.

I'll spell it: B-R-O-W-N.
Ich buchstabiere: B-R-O-W-N.
ikh bookh-shta-BEER-eh: bay-air-o-vay-en.

A	B	C	D	E	F
ah	*bay*	*ts'ay*	*day*	*eh*	*ef*

G	H	I	J	K	L
gay	*ha*	*ee*	*yoht*	*kah*	*el*

M	N	O	P	Q	R
em	*en*	*oh*	*pay*	*koo*	*air*

S	T	U	V	W	X
ess	*tay*	*oo*	*fow*	*vay*	*ix*

Y	Z
IP-see-lohn	*ts'et*

Although some American and English names are fairly easy to say in German, others are often strange to German ears. You will find the spelled-out alphabet very useful for spelling your name when you leave a message.

Where can I make a phone call here?
Wo kann ich hier telefonieren?
vo kahn ikh heer teh-leh-fohn-EER'en?

---

1. Pronounce *ů* like "ee" with your lips in a tight circle.
2. *kh* is a guttural sound.
3. Stress the syllables in capital letters.

Where is a pay phone?
Wo gibt es einen Zahlfernsprecher?
vo ghipt ess INE-en TS'AHL-fairn-shprekh-er?

the telephone book
das Telefonbuch
dahss teh-leh-FOHN-bookh

What kind of coin do I put in?
Was für ein Geldstück muß ich hineintun?
vahss für ine GHELT-shtük moos ikh hin-INE-toon?

Can you change one mark into ten-pfennig pieces for me?
Können Sie mir eine Mark in Zehnpfennigstücke wechseln?
KERN'en zee meer INE-eh mark in
TS'AYN-pfen-nikh-shtük-eh VEX-eln?

And if there is no public telephone available:

May I use your phone?
Dürfte ich Ihr Telefon benutzen?
DÜRF-teh ikh eer teh-leh-FOHN beh-NOOTS'en?

Certainly.	**How much do I owe you?**
Natürlich.	Was schulde ich Ihnen?
na-TÜR-likh.	*vahss SHOOL-deh ikh*
	EEN-en?
Hello, Operator.	**I got a wrong number.**
Hallo Zentrale.	Ich war falsch verbunden.
HA-lo ts'en-TRA-leh.	*ikh var fahlsh*
	fair-BOOND'en.

18. Post Office and Telegrams

One of the first things one does when abroad is to write postcards—**Postkarten**—to friends and relatives. Here is how to mail them. You might also impress your friends by adding a few words in German, which you will find at the end of this section.

Where is the post office?
Wo ist das Postamt?
vo isst dahss POST-amht?

. . . a mailbox?
. . . ein Briefkasten?
. . . ine BREEF-kahst-en?

Five ten-pfennig stamps.
Fünf Zehnpfennigmarken.
fünf TS'AYN-pfen-nikh-MARK-en.

How much is needed?
Wieviel braucht man?
vee-FEEL browkht mahn?

Airmail.
Per Luftpost.
pair LOOFT-post.

For a letter to the United States.
Für einen Brief in die Vereinigten Staaten.
für INE-en breef in dee fair-INE-nikh-ten SHTAHT-en.

For a letter to Canada.
Für einen Brief nach Kanada.
für INE-en breef nakh KA-na-da.

. . . to Spain.
. . . nach Spanien.
. . . nach SHPA-nee-en.

. . . to Holland.
. . . nach Holland.
. . . nakh HOHL-lahnt.

. . . to Russia.
. . . nach Russland.
. . . nakh ROOS-lahnt.

---

1. Pronounce *ü* like "ee" with your lips in a tight circle.
2. *kh* is a guttural sound.
3. Stress the syllables in capital letters.

. . . to England.	**. . . to France.**
. . . nach England.	. . . nach Frankreich.
. . . nakh EHNG-lahnt.	*. . . nakh FRAHNK-rye'kh.*

. . . to Switzerland.	**. . . to Austria.**
. . . in die Schweiz.	. . . nach Österreich.
. . . in dee shvy'ts.	*. . . nakh ER-stair-rye'kh.*

For the names of other selected countries, see the dictionary.

Registered.	**Insured.**
Eingeschrieben.	Versichert.
INE-gheh-shree-ben.	*fair-ZICH-ert.*

Where can I send a telegram?
Wo kann ich ein Telegram abschicken?
Vo kahn ikh ine teh-leh-GRAHM AHP-schick'en?

How much does each syllable cost?
Was kostet die Silbe?
vahss KO-stet dee ZEEL-beh?

I need writing paper.	**Envelopes.**
Ich brauche Schreibpapier.	Briefumschläge.
ikh BROW-khe SHRIBE-pa-PEER.	*BREEF-oom-shleh-gheh.*

Can you lend me a pen?
Können Sie mir einen Kugelschreiber leihen?
KERN'en zee meer INE-en KOO-gel-shry-ber LY'en?

Can you lend me a pencil?
Können Sie mir einen Bleistift leihen?
KERN'en zee meer INE-en BLY-shtift LY'en?

Can you give me some stamps?
Können Sie mir einige Briefmarken geben?
KERN'en zee meer INE-ig-eh BREEF-mark-en GAYB'en?

Postkarten

Dear John,
Lieber Hans,

Dear Jane,
Liebe Johanna,

All best regards from Munich.
Viele Grüße aus München.

This city is beautiful.
Diese Stadt ist sehr schön.

I'm enjoying this trip very much.
Mir gefällt sehr gut diese Reise.

But I miss you very much.
Aber Sie fehlen mir sehr.

I'll be back soon.
Ich werde bald zurückkommen.

Best wishes to everyone.
Die besten Wünsche an alle.

Sincerely,
Herzlichst,

With love!
Allerherzlichst!

Yours, (m)   **Yours, (f)**   **Yours, (pl)**
Ihr,   Ihre,   Ihre,

---

1. Pronounce *ü* like "ee" with your lips in a tight circle.
2. *kh* is a guttural sound.
3. Stress the syllables in capital letters.

19. Seasons and Weather

winter	spring	summer	autumn
Winter	Frühling	Sommer	Herbst
VIN-ter	*FRÜ-ling*	*ZO-mer*	*Hairpst*

How is the weather?
Wie ist das Wetter?
vee isst dahss VET-ter?

The weather is fine.
Das Wetter ist schön.
dahss VET-ter isst shern.

It is raining.
Es regnet.
ess RAYG-net.

I need an umbrella.
Ich brauche einen Regenschirm.
Ikh BROW-kheh INE-en RAY-ghen-sheerm.

. . . a raincoat.
. . . einen Regenmantel.
. . . INE-en RAY-ghen-mahn-tel.

. . . boots.
. . . Stiefel.
. . . SHTEE-fel.

It is cold.
Es ist kalt.
ess isst kahlt.

It's snowing.
Es schneit.
ess shnite.

Do you like to ski?
Laufen Sie gerne Schi?
LOWF'en zee GAIR-neh shee?

. . . to ice-skate?
. . . Schlittschuh?
. . . SHLEET-shoo?

I want to rent skis.
Ich möchte Schier mieten.
ikh MERKH-teh SHEE-er MEET'en.

---

1. Pronounce ů like "ee" with your lips in a tight circle.
2. *kh* is a guttural sound.
3. Stress the syllables in capital letters.

I want to rent ice skates.
Ich möchte Schlittschuhe mieten.
ikh MERKH-teh SHLEET-shoo-eh MEET'en.

It is very hot.
Es ist sehr heiß.
ess isst zair hice.

Let's go swimming!
Gehen wir schwimmen!
GAY'en veer SHVIM'en!

Where is the pool?
Wo ist das Schwimmbad?
vo isst dahss SHVIM-baht?

. . . the beach?
. . . der Strand?
. . . dair shtrahnd?

I want to rent a boat.
Ich mochte ein Boot mieten.
ikh MERKH-teh boat MEET'en.

. . . a windsurfer.
. . . ein Windsurfer.
. . . ine VIND-sur-fer.

. . . air tanks.
. . . Luftflaschen.
. . . LOOFT-flah-shen.

. . . a mask and fins.
. . . eine Maske und Flossen.
. . . EYE-neh MAHS-keh oont FLOHS-sen.

Is it safe to swim here?
Ist es sicher hier zu schwimmen?
isst ess ZIK-her here ts'oo SCHWIMM'en?

Are there sharks?
Gibt ess Haifische?
Ghibt ess HY-fish-heh?

20. Doctor and Dentist

Doctor

I am ill.
Ich bin krank.
ikh bin krahnk.

My wife . . .
Meine Frau . . .
MY-neh frow . . .

My husband . . .
Mein Mann . . .
mine mahn . . .

My daughter . . .
Meine Tochter . . .
MY-neh TOKH-ter . . .

My son . . .
Mein Sohn . . .
mine zohn . . .

My friend . . .
Mein Freund . .
mine froynt . . .

. . . is ill.
. . . ist krank.
. . . isst krahnk.

I don't feel well.
Ich fühle mich nicht wohl.
ikh FÜL-eh mikh nikht vohl.

We need a doctor.
Wir brauchen einen Arzt.
veer BROW-kh'en INE-en artst.

When can he come?
Wann kann er kommen?
vahn kahn air KOHM'en?

Well, what's wrong with you?
Nun, was ist los mit Ihnen?
noon, vahss isst lohss mit EEN-en?

Where does it hurt?
Wo tut es weh?
vo toot ess vay?

Here.
Hier.
heer.

I have a pain . . .
Ich habe Schmerzen . . .
ikh HAHB-eh SHMAIR-ts'en . . .

. . . in the head.
. . . im Kopf.
. . . im kohpf.

---

1. Pronounce *ů* like "ee" with your lips in a tight circle.
2. *kh* is a guttural sound.
3. Stress the syllables in capital letters.

He (she) has a pain . . .　　　　　**. . . in the throat.**
Er (Sie) hat Schmerzen . . .　　　　**. . . im Hals.**
air (zee) haht SHMAIR-ts'en . . .　*. . . im hahlss.*

. . . in the ear.　　**. . . in the stomach.**　　**. . . in the foot.**
. . . im Ohr.　　　. . . im Bauch.　　　. . . im Fuß.
. . . im ohr.　　*. . . im bowkh.*　　*. . . im foos.*

. . . in the back.　　**. . . in the leg.**　　**. . . in the arm.**
. . . im Rücken.　　. . . im Bein.　　. . . im Arm.
. . . im RÜ-ken.　　*. . . im bine.*　　*. . . im arm.*

. . . in the hand.　　　　**I am dizzy.**
. . . in der Hand.　　　　Mir ist schwindlig.
. . . in dair hahnt.　　　*meer isst SHVIND-likh.*

I have a fever.　　　　**I cannot sleep.**
Ich habe Fieber.　　　Ich kann nicht schlafen.
ikh HAHB-eh FEE-ber.　*Ikh kahn nikht SHLAHF'en.*

I have diarrhea.　　　　**Since when?**
Ich habe Durchfall.　　　Seit wann?
ikh HAHB-eh DOORKH-fahl.　*zite vahn?*

Since yesterday.　　　　**For three days.**
Seit gestern.　　　　　Seit drei Tagen.
zite GUESS-tern.　　　*zite dry TAHG-en.*

What have you eaten?　　　　**Undress!**
Was haben sie gegessen?　　　Auskleiden!
vahss HAHB'en zee gheh-GUESS'en?　*OWSS-kly-den!*

Open your mouth!　　　　**Lie down!**
Öffnen Sie den Mund!　　　Legen Sie sich hin!
ERF-nen zee den moont!　　*LAYG'en zee zikh hin!*

Show me your tongue!
Zeigen Sie mir die Zunge!
TS'Y-ghen zee meer dee TS'OONG-eh!

Sit up!
Setzen Sie sich aufrecht!
ZETZ'en zee zikh OWF-rekht!

Cough!
Husten Sie!
HOOST'en zee!

Breathe deeply!
Tief einatmen!
teef INE-aht-men!

Get dressed!
Ziehen Sie sich an!
TS'EE'en zee zikh ahn!

You must stay in bed.
Sie müssen im Bett bleiben.
zee MÜSS'en im bet BLY-ben.

Is it serious?
Ist es schlimm?
isst ess shlim?

You must go to the hospital.
Sie müssen ins Krankenhaus.
zee MÜSS'en inss KRAHNK-en-howss.

Take this prescription.
Nehmen Sie dieses Rezept.
NAYM'en zee DEE-zess reh-TS'EPT.

Take these pills.
Nehmen Sie diese Tabletten
NAYM'en zee DEE-zeh tahb-LET-ten.

No. It isn't serious.
Nein, es ist nicht schlimm.
nine, ess isst nikht shlimm.

Don't worry.
Machen Sie sich keine Sorgen.
MAHKH'en zee zikh KINE-eh ZOR-ghen.

You have . . .
Sie haben . . .
zee HAHB'en . . .

. . . indigestion.
. . . Verdauungsstörungen.
*. . . fair-DOW-oongss-
shter-oong-en.*

---

1. Pronounce ü like "ee" with your lips in a tight circle.
2. *kh* is a guttural sound.
3. Stress the syllables in capital letters.

. . . **an infection.**
. . . eine Enzündung.
. . . *INE-eh ent-TS'ŮN-doong.*

. . . **a cold.**
. . . eine Erkältung.
. . . *INE-eh air-KEL-toong.*

. . . **appendicitis.**
. . . eine Blinddarmentzündung.
. . . *INE-eh BLINT-darm-ent-ts'ůn-döong.*

. . . **a heart attack.**
. . . einen Herzanfall.
. . . *INE-en HAIRTS-ahn-fahl.*

Be careful!
Seien Sie vorsichtig!
ZYE'en zee FOR-zikh-tikh!

Don't eat too much.
Essen Sie nicht zu viel.
ESS'en zee nikht ts'oo feel.

Don't drink any alcohol.
Trinken Sie keinen Alkohol.
TRINK'en zee KINE-en ahl-ko-HOHL.

Except beer, of course.
Außer Bier, natürlich.
OWSS-er beer, na-TŮR-likh.

How do you feel today?
Wie fühlen Sie sich heute?
vee FŮL'en zee zikh HOY-teh?

Badly.
Schlecht.
Shlekht.

Better.
Besser.
BES-ser.

Much better.
Viel besser.
feel BES-ser.

The Centigrade scale is also used to measure body temperature. The normal body temperature is 37°C. So if you have anything higher than that, you have a fever—**Sie haben Fieber.**

Dentist

In the unlikely event that the dentist should hurt you, tell him **Halt, bitte!**—"Stop, please!" or **Einen Augenblick!**—"Wait a moment!" This will give you time to regain your courage.

Can you recommend a dentist to me?
Können Sie mir einen Zahnarzt empfehlen?
KERN-en zee meer INE-en TS'ahn-artst emp-FAIL'en?

I have a toothache.
Ich habe Zahnschmerzen.
ikh HAHB-eh TS'AHN-shmairts-en.

It hurts here.
Es tut hier weh.
ess toot heer vay.

You need a filling.
Sie haben eine Plombe nötig.
zee HAHB'en INE-eh plohm-beh NER-tikh.

There is an inflammation.
Das ist eine Entzündung.
dahss isst INE-eh ent-TS'ŮN-doong.

I must extract this tooth.
Ich muß diesen Zahn ziehen.
Ikh mooss DEE-zen ts'ahn TS'EE'en.

How long will it take?
Wie lange wird es dauern?
vee LAHNG-eh veert ess DOW-ern?

A few minutes.
Einige Minuten.
EYE-nig-eh mee-NOO-ten.

An injection against pain, please.
Eine Spritze gegen Schmerzen, bitte.
INE-eh SHPRITS-eh GAY-ghen SHMAIRTS-en, BIT-teh.

---

1. Pronounce *ů* like "ee" with your lips in a tight circle.
2. *kh* is a guttural sound.
3. Stress the syllables in capital letters.

Just fix it temporarily.
Machen Sie es provisorisch.
MAKH'en zee ess pro-vee-ZOHR-ish.

Does it hurt?
Tut es weh?
toot ess vay?

No, not at all.
Nein, überhaupt nicht.
nine, Ü-ber-howpt nikht.

Yes, a little.
Ja, ein bißchen.
ya, ine BISS-yen.

Thank you.
Danke.
DAHN-keh.

Is that all?
Ist das alles?
isst dahss AH-less?

How much do I owe you?
Wieviel bin ich Ihnen schuldig?
vee-FEEL bin ikh EEN-en SHOOL-dikh?

21. Problems and Police

Although the situations suggested below may never happen to you, the words are useful to know, just in case!

Go away!
Gehen Sie weg!
GAY'en zee vek!

Leave me alone!
Lassen Sie mich allein!
LAHSS'en zee mikh ahl-LINE.

Or I'll call a policeman.
Oder ich rufe die Polizei.
OH-dair ikh ROOF-eh dee po-lee-TS'EYE.

Police!
Polizei!
pol-lee-TS'EYE!

Help!
Hilfe!
HEEL-feh!

What's going on?
Was ist los?
vahss isst lohss?

This man is annoying me.
Dieser Mann belästigt mich.
DEE-zair mahn beh-LESS-tikt mikh.

Where is the police station?
Wo ist die Polizeiwache?
vo isst dee po-lee-TS'EYE-vakh-eh?

I have been robbed.
Man hat mich beraubt.
mahn haht mikh beh-R'OWPT.

My watch . . .
Meine Uhr . . .
MINE-eh oor . . .

My wallet . . .
Mine Geldtasche . . .
MINE-eh GHELT-tahsh-eh . . .

My jewelry . . .
Mein Schmuck . . .
mine shmook . . .

My car . . .
Mein Wagen . . .
mine VA-ghen . . .

. . . has been stolen.
. . . ist gestohlen worden.
. . . isst gheh-SHTOHL'en VOR-den.

---

1. Pronounce *ŭ* like "ee" with your lips in a tight circle.
2. *kh* is a guttural sound.
3. Stress the syllables in capital letters.

131

I've lost my suitcase (my passport).
Ich habe meinen Koffer (meinen Pass) verloren.
ikh HA-beh MY-nen KO-fair (MY-nen pahss) fair-LOR'en.

Stop!	**That's the one!**
Halt!	Das ist er!
hahlt!	*dahss isst air!*

I am innocent.
Ich bin unschuldig.
ikh bin oon-SHOOL-dikh.

I haven't done anything.
Ich habe nichts getan.
ikh HAHB-eh nikhts gheh-TAHN.

I don't recognize him.
Ich erkenne ihn nicht.
ikh air-KEN-neh een nikht.

I need a lawyer.
Ich brauche einen Anwalt.
ikh BROW-kheh INE-en AHN-vahlt.

Notify the American Consulate.
Benachrichtigen Sie das amerikanische Konsulat.
ben-NAHKH-rikh-tee-ghen zee dahss ah-meh-ree-KAHN-ish-eh kohn-soo-LAHT.

It's nothing.	**It's a misunderstanding.**
Es ist nichts.	Es ist ein Mißverständnis.
es isst nikhts.	*ess isst ine MISS-fair-shtend-niss.*

Don't worry!	**May I go?**
Keine Sorgen!	Darf ich gehen?
KINE-eh ZORG-en!	*darf ikh GAY'en?*

22. Housekeeping

The following chapter will be especially interesting for those who plan to stay longer in Germany, Austria, or Switzerland, or have occasion to employ German-speaking babysitters or household help, abroad or even at home.

What is your name?
Wie ist Ihr Name?
vee isst eer NA-meh?

Can you cook?
Können Sie kochen?
KERN'en zee KOKH'en?

Where did you work before?
Wo haben Sie vorher gearbeitet?
vo HAHB'en zee FOR-hair gheh-AR-by-tet?

Can you take care of a baby?
Können Sie auf ein Baby aufpassen?
KERN'en zee owf ine BAY-bee OWF-pahs-sen?

We will pay you _____ marks per week.
Wir zahlen Ihren _____ Mark pro Woche.
veer TS'AHL'en EER-en _____ mark pro VO-khe.

Thursday is your day off.
Donnerstag ist Ihr freier Tag.
DOHN-erss-tahk isst eer FRY-er tahk.

This is your room.
Das ist Ihr Zimmer.
dahss isst eer TS'IM-er.

Please clean . . .
Bitte reinigen Sie . . .
BIT-teh RYE-nee-ghen zee . . .

. . . the living room.
. . . das Wohnzimmer.
. . . dahss VOHN-ts'im-er.

. . . the bathroom.
. . . das Badezimmer.
. . . dahss BA-deh-ts'im-er.

. . . the kitchen.
. . . die Küche.
. . . dee KÜKH-eh.

---

1. Pronounce *ü* like "ee" with your lips in a tight circle.
2. *kh* is a guttural sound.
3. Stress the syllables in capital letters.

. . . the bedroom.	. . . the dining room.
. . . das Schlafzimmer.	. . . das Eßzimmer.
. . . dahss SHLAHF-ts'im-er.	. . . dahss ESS-ts'im-er.

Use the vacuum cleaner.
Nehmen Sie den Staubsauger.
NEH-men zee den SHT'OWB-z'ow-gher.

Wash the dishes.	**Sweep the floor.**
Spülen Sie das Geschirr.	Kehren Sie den Fußboden.
SHPÜL'en zee dahss gheh-SHEER.	*KAIR'en zee den FOOSS-bo-den.*

Polish the silver.	**Iron this.**
Putzen Sie das Silber.	Bügeln Sie dies.
POOTS'en zee dahss ZEEL-ber.	*BÜ-gheln zee deess.*

Make the beds.	**Change the sheets.**
Machen Sie die Betten.	Wechseln Sie die Laken.
MAKH'en zee dee BET-en.	*VEX-eln zee dee LAHK-en.*

Wash this.	**Use bleach.**
Waschen Sie dies.	Benutzen Sie Bleichmittel.
VA-shen zee deess.	*BEH-noots'en zee BLY'KH-mit-tel.*

Have you done it already?
Haben Sie es schon gemacht?
HAHB'en zee ess shohn gheh-MAKHT?

Put the meat in the refrigerator.
Legen Sie das Fleisch in den Kühlschrank.
LAYG'en zee dahss fly'sh in den KÜL-shrahnk.

Go to the market.	**Here is the list.**
Gehen Sie zum Markt.	Hier ist die Liste.
GAY'en zee ts'oom markt.	*heer isst dee LEES-teh.*

If someone calls, write the name here.
Wenn jemand anruft, schreiben Sie hier den Namen auf.
ven YEH-mahnt AHN-rooft, SHRY-ben zee heer den
   NA-men owf.

I can be reached at this number.
Ich bin unter dieser Nummer zu erreichen.
ikh bin OONT-er DEE-zer NOOM-er ts'oo air-RYE-khen.

I'll be back at four o'clock.
Ich bin um vier Uhr wieder zurück.
ikh bin oom feer oor VEE-der ts'oo-RŮK.

Give the child its food at one o'clock.
Geben Sie dem Kind sein Essen um eins.
GAYB'en zee dem kint zine ESS-en oom ine'ts.

Give the child a bath.
Baden Sie das Kind.
BAHD'en zee dahss kint.

Put him to bed at eight o'clock.
Bringen Sie es um acht Uhr ins Bett.
BRING'en zee ess oom akht oor inss bet.

Serve lunch at two o'clock.
Bringen Sie das Mittagessen um zwei Uhr.
BRING'en zee dahss MIT-takh-ess-en oom ts'vy oor.

This evening we are having guests.
Heute Abend haben wir Gäste.
HOY-teh AH-bent HAHB'en veer GUESS-teh.

Serve dinner at nine o'clock.
Servieren Sie das Abendessen um neun Uhr.
sair-VEER'en zee dahss AH-bent-ess-en oom noyn oor.

---

1. Pronounce *ů* like "ee" with your lips in a tight circle.
2. *kh* is a guttural sound.
3. Stress the syllables in capital letters.

23. Some Business Phrases

You will find the short phrases and vocabulary in this section extremely useful if you are on a business trip to Germany, Austria, or Switzerland. While it is true that English is a prominent foreign language in Central Europe and that efficient interpreters are available, these phrases will add another dimension to your contacts with your German-speaking business associates. The fact that you have made the effort to master some business expressions will be a compliment to your hosts.

Good morning. Is Mr. Schwarz in?
Guten Morgen. Ist Hr. Schwarz da?
GOOT'en MOR-ghen. isst hair shvarts da?

I have an appointment with him.
Ich habe mit ihm eine Verabredung.
ikh HA-beh mitt eem INE-eh vair-AHB-reh-doong.

Here is my card.
Hier ist meine Karte.
here isst MY-neh KAR-teh.

Thank you. He is expecting you.
Danke. Er erwarte Sie.
DAHN-keh. air ehr-VAR-teh zee.

Welcome to Germany, Mr. Brown.
Wilkommen in Deutschland, Hr. Brown.
vill-KOM-men in DOYTCH-lahnt, hair brown.

---

1. Pronounce ů like "ee" with your lips in a tight circle.
2. *kh* is a guttural sound.
3. Stress the syllables in capital letters.

How do you like Munich?
Wie gefällt Ihnen München?
vee ghe-FAYLT EE-nen MŮNCH-yen?

Very much. It's a marvelous city.
Sehr gut. Es ist eine herrliche Stadt.
zair goot. es isst INE-eh HAIR-lick-heh shtaht.

We understand that . . .
Wir verstehen daß . . .
veer fair-SHTEH'en dahss . . .

. . . you are interested in our cars.
. . . Sie sich für unsere Wagen interessieren.
. . . zee zikh fǔr OON-seh-reh VA-ghen in-teh-reh-SEER'en.

Here is our latest catalog.
Hier ist unsere neuste Broschure.
here isst OON-zeh-reh NOY-steh bro-SHŮR-reh.

It shows all our new models,
Es zeigt alle unsere neuen Modellen,
ess ts'ygt AHL-leh OON-zeh-reh NOY-en mo-DEL-len,

. . . limousines, two-door, and four-door cars,
. . . Limosinen, Zwei-türe und Vier-türe Wagonen,
. . . lee-mo-ZEE-nen, ts'vy TǓ-reh oont FEER-tǔr va-GO-nen,

. . . convertibles and sports cars.
. . . Cabriolets und Sportwagen.
. . . ca-bree'o-LAY oont SHPORT-va-ghen.

Thank you.	**That's just what I need.**
Danke.	Das ist genau was ich brauche.
DAHN-keh.	*Dahss isst geh-NOW vahss ikh BROW-kheh.*

Would you like to inspect our plant?
Möchten Sie unser Werk besichtigen?
MERK-ten zee OON-zair vairk beh-ZIKH-tih-ghen?

A very good idea!
Eine sehr gute Idee!
INE-eh zair GOO-teh EE-day!

That is very kind of you.
Das ist sehr freundlich von Ihnen.
dahss isst zair FROYND-likh fohn EE-nen.

It was a pleasure to visit your factory.
Es war eine Vergnügen Ihre Fabrik zu besuchen.
*ess var INE-eh fairg-NÜ-ghen EE-reh fa-BREEK t'soo
   beh-ZOO-khen.*

It's very efficient.
Es ist sehr leistungsfähig.
ess isst zair LICE-toongs-fay-hig.

We would like to place an order.
Wir möchten bei Ihnen bestellen.
Veer MERK-ten by EE-nen beh-SHTELL'en.

We expect a discount of _____ percent.
Wir erwarten einen Rabatt von _____ prozent.
*veer air-VART'en EYE-nen ra-BAHT fohn _____ pro-
   TS'ENT.*

What are your terms of payment?
Was sind Ihre Zahlesbedingungen?
vahss zint EE-reh TS'AH-less-beh-DING-ung-en?

---

1. Pronounce *ü* like "ee" with your lips in a tight circle.
2. *kh* is a guttural sound.
3. Stress the syllables in capital letters.

By thirty-day bank draft.
Mit Banküberweisung von dreißig Tagen.
mitt bahnk-Ü-bair-vy-zoong fohn DRY-sikh TA-ghen.

Irrevocable letter of credit.
Unwiederrufbarer Kreditbrief.
oon-vee-dehr-ROOF-bar'er kreh-DEET-brief.

What is your delivery time?
Wie lange ist Ihre Lieferzeit?
vee LAHN-ghe isst EE-reh LEE-fair-ts'ite?

Are these your best terms?
Sind das Ihre besten Bedingungen?
zint dahss EE-reh BESS-ten be-DING-oon-ghen?

But of course! We have given you . . .
Aber sicher! Wir haben Ihnen . . .
AH-bair ZIK-hair! Veer HAHB'en EE-nen . . .

. . . the best possible dealer's discount.
. . . den bestmöglichen Händlerrabatt gegeben.
. . . den best-MERG-lik'en hend-ler-ra-BAHT ghe-GAYB'en.

Would you like to sign the contract now?
Möchten Sie jetzt den Vertrag unterschreiben?
MERK-ten zee yetzt den fair-TRAHK OON-tair-shryb'en?

We're in agreement, aren't we?
Wir sind einverstanden, nicht wahr?
veer zint INE-fair-shtahn-den, nikht var?

We need time to examine the contract.
Wir benütigen Zeit den Vertrag zu prufen.
veer beh-NÜ-teeg'en ts'ite den fair-TRAHK ts'oo PRUF'en.

Our lawyers will get in contact with you.
Unsere Anwälte werden sich bei Ihnen melden.
OONT-seh-reh ahn-VEL-teh VAIRD'en zikh by EE-nen
  MELD'en.

It's a pleasure to be able to do business with you.
Es freut uns mit Ihnen Geschäfte machen zu können.
ess froyt oonts mitt EE-nen gheh-SHAYF-teh MA-khen
  ts'oo KER-nen.

We would like to invite you to dinner.
Wir möchten Sie gerne zum Abendessen einladen.
veer MERK-ten zee GAIR-neh ts'oom AH-bent-ess'en
  INE-lahd'en.

Can we call for you at eight?
Können wir Sie um acht Uhr abholen?
KER-nen veer zee oom ahkt oor AHB-hohl'en?

Many thanks for the invitation.
Vielen Dank für die Einladung.
FEEL-en dahnk für dee INE-la-doong.

. . . **for the dinner.**	. . . **for everything.**
. . . für das Essen.	. . . für alles.
. . . für dahss ES-sen.	*. . . für AHL-less.*

I was very happy to meet you.
Es hat mich sehr gefreut Sie können zu lernen.
ess haht mikh zair gheh-FROYT zee KER-nen ts'oo
  LAIRN'en.

If you come to America,
Wenn Sie nach Amerika kommen,
ven zee nahkh ah-MEH-ree-ka KOHM'en,

---

1. Pronounce *ü* like "ee" with your lips in a tight circle.
2. *kh* is a guttural sound.
3. Stress the syllables in capital letters.

let me know,
lassen Sie mich wissen,
LAHS'en zee mikh VISS'en,

so that we can receive you equally well.
so daß wir Sie ebenso gut empfangen können.
*zo dahss veer zee EH-ben-zo goot emp-FAHNG'en
  KER-nen.*

24. A New Type of Dictionary

This dictionary supplies a list of English words with their translation into German. Only one German equivalent is given for each English word—the one most immediately useful to you—so you won't be in doubt regarding which word to use. The phonetic pronunciation is also given for each word so that you will have no difficulty in being understood.

Below we have detailed some suggestions and shortcuts that will enable you to use this dictionary to make hundreds of correct and useful sentences by yourself.

Each German noun is either masculine, feminine, or neuter, and this affects the form of any adjectives and articles that are used in front of it. In the dictionary we have indicated the gender of each noun by putting the proper form of the word "the" in front of it in parentheses: **der** for masculine nouns, **die** for feminine, and **das** for neuter. In the plural, "the" is **die** before a noun of any gender (when it is used as the subject of a sentence).

In the case of nouns referring to people, we have given two forms—one referring to men and one to women:

the foreigner **(der) Ausländer** (a man)
(die) Ausländerin (a woman)

The plural of nouns, except of a few of foreign origin, is not made with an "s" as in English but by adding one of the endings **-e, -er, -n,** or **-en,** and sometimes by changing a simple vowel within the noun to an "umlaut" (**ä, ö,** or **ü**). In this dictionary the plural ending for each noun is given after a slash. Thus **Wohnung/-en** means that the plural of **Wohnung** is **Wohnungen,** and **Arm/-e** that the plural of **Arm** is **Arme.** When an umlaut is used, the entire word, or the part of the word in which the umlaut occurs, is repeated for the plural: **Kunst/Künste.** A dash after the slash mark means that the plural form of the word is just the same as the singular: **Keller/–** means that the plural of **Keller** is also

Keller (just as a few English words, such as "sheep" and "deer," have the same form for the singular and plural).

Adjectives are used in their simple form without any special ending when they come after the noun to which they refer:

The house is small.   **Das Haus ist klein.**

When an adjective comes before its noun, either without an article or with the article **ein** (masculine or neuter) or **eine** (feminine), "a," it must take the appropriate masculine, feminine, or neuter ending. These endings, which are listed for your convenience after each adjective in the dictionary, are **-er, -e,** and **-es** respectively when the noun is used as the subject of the sentence.

a small garden   **ein kleiner Garten**
a small apartment   **eine kleine Wohnung**
a small house   **ein kleines Haus**

When the noun is preceded by the article **der, die,** or **das,** "the," ending of the adjective is **-e** for all three genders.

the small garden   **der kleine Garten**
the small apartment   **die kleine Wohnung**
the small house   **das kleine Haus**

The forms of the articles and the endings of the adjectives also vary when the noun is used as a direct or indirect object or in the possessive case. You have, no doubt, already noticed that the endings change in the phrase book; now you know why. Such case endings for the articles can be found in the dictionary itself, under entries like "at the," "to the," "in the," "on the," etc.

The first form of the adjective given in the dictionary is also the adverb. Both adjectives and adverbs form comparatives by adding the ending **-er:**

quick, *or* quickly   **schnell**
quicker, *or* more quickly   **schneller**

Verbs are given in the dictionary in their infinitive form, ending in **-en.** Observe how the ending of the verb changes according to the subject:

(to) go	**gehen**
I go (*or* am going)	**ich gehe**
you (familiar) go	**du gehst**
he, she, it goes	**er, sie, es geht**
we, you (formal), they go	**wir, Sie, sie gehen**

(Notice that the same verb form is used with any of the subjects "we," "you," or "they.") Although two forms are given for "you," you should concentrate on using **Sie,** since it is much more polite than **du,** which is used within the family, among close friends and students, and to children.

Some of the verbs in the dictionary are followed by (SP) to indicate that they have a separable prefix. These verbs simply "split" when used in forms other than the infinitive. For instance:

to come in	*herein***kommen** (SP)
Come in!	**Kommen Sie** *herein!*

A detailed study of German verbs is not within the scope of this book. But to help you in making sentences, the present tense of some of the most important verbs—such as "to be," "to have," "to go," "to come," "to want"—is given in this dictionary, as well as some of the most important past participles. In addition, here are some helpful hints to enable you to form sentences with some of the other basic verb forms (tenses and moods), since you have already seen how the present tense is generally formed.

To give an order, use the infinitive form followed by **Sie:**

to go	**gehen**
Go!	**Gehen Sie!**

To say that you want to do something or to invite someone to do something, use "to want" (**will** or **wollen**) with the infinitive of the second verb:

| I want to go. | **Ich will gehen.** |
| Do you want to go? | **Wollen Sie gehen?** |

For the negative use **nicht** (''not'') before the verb:

| I do not want to go. | **Ich will nicht gehen.** |

And for ''would like (to) . . .''—

| I would like (to) . . . | **Ich möchte . . .** |
| Would you like . . . ? | **Möchten Sie . . . ?** |

To express the future, use the present tense of **werden** (''to become'') with the infinitive form of the verb:

I will come	**ich werde kommen**
you (familiar) will come	**du wirst kommen**
he, she, it will come	**er, sie, es wird kommen**
we, you (formal), they will come	**wir, Sie, sie werden kommen**

To express something that happened in the past, for most verbs given in the dictionary use the present tense of **haben** (''to have'') with the past participle of the verb:

| I had, *or* I have had | **ich habe gehabt** |
| I saw, *or* I have seen | **ich habe gesehen** |

A few verbs require that you use the present tense of **sein** (''to be'') with the past participle. These are mostly verbs that express ideas of coming or going, arriving or leaving, etc.:

he went, *or* he has gone   **er ist gegangen**

Since only the most important or irregular past participles are given in the dictionary, note that they are generally formed by adding the prefix **ge-** and changing the ending **-en** of the infinitive to **-t**, or else leaving the **-en** and changing the internal spelling of the word. (Notice that the past participle is usually the very last word in the sentence.)

(to) do	**machen**
I have done it.	**Ich habe es gemacht.**

(to) find	**finden**
She found it.	**Sie hat es gefunden.**

Object pronouns are given within the alphabetical order of the dictionary. They usually come after the verb, as in English:

Tell me.	**Sagen Sie mir.**
Don't tell him.	**Sagen Sie ihm nicht.**
I see him.	**Ich sehe ihn.**

The possessive case of proper names follows the English pattern but without the apostrophe:

Goethe's works   **Goethes Werke**

The possessive forms of the articles and the pronoun can be found within the dictionary.

With this advice and the suggestions given in the dictionary, you will be able to use this communicating dictionary to make up countless sentences on your own and to converse with anyone you may meet.

There is, of course, much more to German grammar than what we have just mentioned in this introduction. There are other tenses and moods, strong and weak verbs, declensions of nouns and adjectives, reflexive pronouns, etc., as well as numerous idiomatic expressions and various sayings which reflect the customs, philosophy, and history of the German-speaking peoples. But you can effectively use the selected basic vocabulary in this dictionary as an important step or even springboard to the mastery of German, and, by means of enthusiastic practice, gradually absorb and constantly improve your command of this rich and expressive language.

A

a, an	ein (m), eine (f), ein (n)	*ine, INE-eh, ine*
able	fähig, -er, -e, -es	*FAY-ikh*
about (concerning)	über	*Ů-ber*
above	über	*Ů-ber*
absent	abwesend	*AHP-vay-zent*
accept	*an*nehmen (SP)	*AHN-nay-men*
accident	(der) Unfall/ Unfälle	*OON-fahl*
accidentally	zufällig	*ts'oo-FEL-likh*
across	über	*Ů-ber*
actor	(der) Schau- spieler/–	*SH'OW-shpeel-er*
actress	(die) Schau- spielerin/-nen	*SH'OW-shpeel-er-in*
address	(die) Adresse /-n	*ah-DRESS-eh*
admission	(der) Eintritt/-e	*INE-trit*
advertisement	(die) An- zeige/-n	*AHN-ts'y-gheh*
advise	raten	*RAHT'en*
afraid	bange	*BAHNG-eh*
I am afraid	Ich fürchte mich	*ikh FŮRKH-teh mikh*
Africa	(das) Afrika	*AH-free-ka*
African	afrikanisch, -er, -e, es	*ah-free-KAHN-ish*

African (person)	(der) Afri-kaner/–	*ah-freeKAHN-er*
	(die) Afrika-nerin/-nen	*ah-free-KAHN-er-in*
after	nach	*nahkh*
afternoon	(der) Nach-mittag/-e	*NAHKH-mit-tahk*
again	wieder	*VEE-der*
against	gegen	*GAY-ghen*
age	(das) Alter	*AHLT-er*
agent	(der) Agent/-en	*ah-ghent*
ago	vor (See how it is used on page 26)	*for*
agree	*über*einstimmen (SP)	*ŭ-ber-INE-shtimm'en*
agreed!	abgemacht!	*AHP-gheh-makht!*
ahead	vorne	*FOR-neh*
air	(die) Luft	*looft*
air conditioning	(die) Klimaan-lage/-en	*KLEE-ma-ahn-la-gheh*
airmail	(die) Luftpost	*LOOFT-post*
airplane	(das) Flug-zeug/-e	*FLOOK-ts'oyk*
airport	(der) Flug-platz/-plätze	*FLOOK-plahtz*
all	alle	*AHL-eh*
That's all!	Das ist alles!	*dahss isst AHL-less!*
allow	erlauben	*air-L'OW-ben*

all right	gut	*goot*
almost	beinahe	*by-NA-eh*
alone	allein	*ahl-LINE*
already	schon	*shohn*
also	auch	*owkh*
(to) alter	ändern	*END-ern*
although	obwohl	*ohp-VOHL*
always	immer	*IM-mer*
(I) am	(Ich) bin	*(ikh) bin*
America	Amerika	*ah-MAY-ree-ka*
American	amerikanisch, -er, -e, -es	*ah-may-ree-KAHN-ish*
American (person)	(der) Amerikaner/–	*ah-may-ree-KAHN-er*
	(die) Amerikanerin	*ah-may-ree-KAHN-er-in*
amusing	amüsant, -er, -e, -es	*ah-mü-ZAHNT*
and	und	*oont*
angry	böse, -r, –, -s	*BERZ-eh*
animal	(das) Tier/-e	*teer*
ankle	(der) Fußknöchel/–	*FOOSS-kner-khel*
annoying	ärgerlich, -er, -e, -es	*AIR-gher-likh*
answer	(die) Antwort/-en	*AHNT-vort*
(to) answer	antworten	*AHNT-vort'en*
antiseptic (adv & adj)	antiseptisch, -er, -es, -e	*ahn-tee-SEP-tish*

any (of)	etwas	*ET-vahss*
anyone	irgendwer	*eer-gent-VAIR*
anything	irgend etwas	*eer-ghent et-VAHSS*
anywhere	irgendwo	*EER-ghent-vo*
apartment	(die) Woh-nung/-en	*VO-noong*
appointment	(die) Verabre-dung/-en	*fair-AHP-ray-doong*
April	(der) April	*ahp-REEL*
Arab (person)	(der) Araber/– (die) Arab-erin/-nen	*ah-RAHB-er* *ah-RAHB-er-in*
Arabian	arabisch, -er, -e, -es	*ah-RAHB-ish*
architecture	(die) Archi-tektur	*ar-khee-tek-TOOR*
are		
you (we, they) are	Sie (wir, sie) sind	*zee (veer, zee) zint*
there are	es gibt	*ess ghipt*
arm	(der) Arm/-e	*arm*
army	(die) Armee/-n	*ar-MAY*
around (sur-rounding)	rundherum	*roont-hair-OOM*
around (approxi-mately)	ungefähr	*OON-gheh-fair*
arrival	(die) Ankunft /Ankünfte	*AHN-koonft*
(to) arrive	*an*kommen (SP)	*AHN-kohm'en*
art	(die) Kunst/ Künste	*koonst*

artist	(der) Künstler/–	*KŮNST-ler*
	(die) Künstlerin/-nen	*KŮNST-ler-in*
as	wie	*vee*
as (while)	als	*ahlss*
Asia	Asien	*AH-zee-en*
Asian	asiatisch, -er, -e, -es	*ah-zee-AH-tish*
(to) ask	fragen	*FRAHG'en*
aspirin	*Aspirin*	*ahs-pee-REEN*
assortment	(die) Auswahl /-en	*OWSS-vahl*
at (time)	um	*oom*
at (place)	in	*in*
at the	an dem *or* am (m, n)	*ahn daim, ahm*
	an der	*ahn dair*
	an den	*ahn den*
Atlantic	Atlantik	*aht-LAHN-tick*
Attention!	Achtung!	*AKH-toong!*
August	(der) August	*(dair) OW-goost*
aunt	(die) Tante/-n	*(dee) TAHN-te*
Australia	(das) Australien	*ow-STRA-lee-en*
Australian	australisch, -er, -e, -es	*ow-STRA-lish*
Australian (person)	(der) Australier/–	*ow-STRA-lee-er*
	(die) Australierin/-nen	*ow-STRA-lee-er-in*

Austria	(das) Öster-reich	*ER-ster-ry'kh*
Austrian	österreichisch, -er, -e, -es	*ER-ster-ry'kh-ish*
Austrian (person)	(der) Öster-reicher/–	*ER-ster-ry'kh-er*
	(die) Öster-reicherin /-nen	*ER-ster-ry'kh-er-in*
author	(der) Autor/-en	*ow-TOR*
automatic	automatisch, -er, -e, es	*ow-toh-MA-tish*
automobile	(das) Auto/-s	*OW-toh*
autumn	(der) Herbst	*hair'pst*
avoid	vermeiden	*fair-MY-den*
away	weg	*veck*

B

baby	(das) Kind-chen/–	*KINT-khen*
bachelor	(der) Jung-geselle/-n	YOONG-gheh-zel-le
back (adv.)	zurück	*ts'oo-RŬK*
back (part of the body)	(der) Rücken /–	*RŬK-en*
backward	rückwärts	*RŬK-vairts*
bad	schlecht	*shlekht*
baggage	(das) Gepäck	*ghe-PAYK*
bandage	(die) Binde/-n	*BIN-deh*
bank	(die) Bank/-en	*bahnk*

bar	(die) Bar/-s	*bar*
barber	(der) Friseur /-e	*free-ZERR*
basement	(der) Keller/–	*KELL-er*
bath	(das) Bad /Bäder	*baht*
bathing suit	(der) Badean- zug/-anzüge	*BA-deh-ahn-ts'ook*
bathroom	(das) Bade- zimmer/–	*BA-deh-ts'im-er*
battery	(die) Batterie /-n	*baht-teh-REE*
battle	(die) Schlacht /-en	*shlakht*
(to) be	sein	*zine*

(See also "am," "is," "are," "was," "were," "been.")

beach	(der) Strand /Strände	*shtrahnt*
bear	(der) Bär/-en	*bair*
beard	(der) Bart /Bärte	*bahrt*
beautiful	schön	*shern*
beauty	(die) Schön- heit/-en	*SHERN-hite*
beauty parlor	(der) Schön- heitssalon/-s	*SHERN-hites-sa-lohn*
because	weil	*vile*
bed	(das) Bett/-en	*bet*
bedroom	(das) Schlaf- zimmer/–	*SHLAHF-ts'im-er*

beef	(das) Rind-fleisch	*RINT-fly'sh*
been	gewesen	*gheh-VAY-zen*
beer	(das) Bier	*beer*
before (earlier)	vorher	*FOR-hair*
before (in front of, preceding)	vor, ehe, bevor	*for, AY-eh, beh-FOR*
(to) begin	*an*fangen (SP)	*AHN-fahng'en*
behind	hinter	*HIN-ter*
(to) believe	glauben	*GL'OWB'en*
Belgium	(das) Belgien	*BEL-ghee-en*
Belgian	belgisch, -er, -e, -es	*BEL-ghish*
Belgian (person)	(der) Belgier/– (die) Belgier-in	*BEL-ghee-er BEL-ghee-er-in*
below (prep)	unter	*OON-ter*
below (adv)	unten	*OON-ten*
belt	(der) Gürtel/–	*GUR-tel*
beside	neben	*NAY-ben*
best (adj)	best, bester, beste, bestes	*BEST-er*
best (adv)	am besten	*ahm BEST-en*
(the) best	(das) Beste	*BEST-eh*
best wishes	(die) Glück-wünsche	*GLÜK-vůn-sheh*
better	besser, -er, -e, -es	*BESS-er*
between	zwischen	*TS'VISH-en*

bicycle	(das) Fahrrad /-räder	*FAR-raht*
big	groß, großer, -e, -es	*gross*
bill	(die) Rech- nung/-en	*REKH-noong*
bird	(der) Vogel /Vögel	*FOHG-el*
birthday	(der) Geburts- tag/-e	*ghe-BOORTS-tahk*
black	schwarz, -er, -e, -es	*shvartz*
blanket	(die) Bett- decke/-n	*BET-deck-eh*
blood	(das) Blut	*bloot*
blouse	(die) Bluse/-n	*BLOO-zeh*
blue	blau, -er, -e, -es	*bl'ow*
boardinghouse	(die) Pension	*pen-Z'YOHN*
boat	(das) Boot/-e	*boat*
body	(der) Körper/–	*KERP-er*
book	(das) Buch/ Bücher	*bookh*
bookstore	(die) Buchhand- lung/-en	*BOOKH-hahnd-loong*
born	geboren	*gheh-BORE'en*
(to) borrow	borgen	*BORG'en*
boss	(der) Chef/-s	*shef*
both	beide	*BY-deh*
(to) bother	stören	*SHTERR'en*
bottle	(die) Flasche/-n	*FLA-sheh*

bottom	(der) Boden/ Böden	*BO-den*
bought	gekauft	*gheh-KOWFT*
bowl	(die) Schüs- sel/-n	*SHÜ-sel*
boy	(der) Knabe/-n	*K'NAHB-eh*
brain	(das) Gehirn	*gheh-HEERN*
brake	(die) Bremse/-n	*BREM-ze*
brave	tapfer, -er, -e, -es	*TAHP-fer*
bread	(das) Brot/-e	*broht*
(to) break	brechen	*BREHKH'en*
breakfast	(das) Früh- stück/-e	*FRÜ-shtuk*
bridge	(die) Brücke/-n	*BRÜ-keh*
bridge (card game)	(das) Bridge- spiel/-e	*BRIDGE-shpeel*
briefcase	(die) Akten- tasche/-n	*AHKT-en-ta-sheh*
(to) bring	bringen	*BRING'en*
Bring me . . . (something)	Bringen Sie mir . . .	*BRING'en zee meer . . .*
broken	gebrochen	*gheh-BROKH'en*
brother	(der) Bruder /Brüder	*BROOD-er*
brother-in-law	(der) Schwager /Schwäger	*SHVA-gher*
brown	braun, -er, -e, es	*brown*
brush	(die) Bürste/-n	*(dee) BÜR-steh*

building	(das) Ge-bäude/–	*gheh-BOY-de*
bureau	(das) Büro/-s	*bü-RO*
bus	(der) Bus/-e	*booss*
bus stop	(die) Bushal-testelle/-n	*BOOSS-hahl-teh-shtel-eh*
business	(das) Geschäft/-e	*gheh-SHEFT*
busy	beschäftigt	*beh-SHEFT-ikht*
but	aber	*AH-ber*
butter	(die) Butter	*BOOT-ter*
button	(der) Knopf /Knöpfe	*k'nopf*
(to) buy	kaufen	*KOWF'en*
by (near)	bei	*by*
by (agent)	von	*fohn*

C

cabbage	(der) Kohl	*kohl*
cake	(der) Kuchen/–	*KOO-khen*
(to) call	rufen	*ROOF'en*
(to) call (tele-phone)	*an*rufen (SP)	*AHN-roof'en*
Call me!	Rufen Sie mich an!	*ROOF'en zee mikh ahn!*
calm	ruhig, -er, -e, -es	*ROO-ikh*
camera	(die) Ka-mera/-s	*KA-meh-ra*

can (to be able to)	Können	*KERN'en*
Can you . . . ?	Können Sie . . . ?	*KERN'en zee . . . ?*
I can	ich kann	*ikh kahn*
I can't	ich kann nicht	*ikh kahn nikht*
can (container)	(die) Büchse/-n	*BŮK-seh*
can opener	(der) Büchsen-öffner/–	*BŮK-sen-erf-ner*
capable	fähig, -er, -e, -es	*FAY-ikh*
captain (sea)	(der) Kapitän /-e	*ka-pee-TAIN*
captain (police, army)	(der) Haupt-mann /-männer	*HOWPT-mahn*
car	(der) Wagen/–	*VA-ghen*
carburetor	(der) Ver-gaser/–	*fer-GA-zer*
card	(die) Karte/-n	*KAR-teh*
careful	vorsichtig, -er, -e, -es	*FOR-zikh-tikh*
(Be) careful!	(Seien Sie) vor-sichtig!	*ZY'en zee FOR-zikh-tikh!*
care	(die) Sorge/-n	*ZOR-gheh*
carrot	(die) Karot-te/-n	*ka-ROHT-eh*
(to) carry	tragen	*TRAHG'en*
Carry this to . . . !	Tragen Sie dies zu . . . !	*TRAHG'en zee deess ts'oo . . . !*

castle	(das) Schloß/ Schlösser	*shlohss*
cat	(die) Katze/-n	*KAHT-ts'eh*
cathedral	(der) Dom/-e	*dohm*
Catholic	katholisch, -er, -e, -es	*ka-TOH-lish*
cellar	(der) Keller/–	*KELL-er*
cemetery	(der) Fried- hof/-höfe	*FREED-hohf*
center	(das) Zent- rum/-s	*TS'ENT-room*
centimeter	(der) Zenti- meter/–	*ts'en-tee-MAYT-er*
century	(das) Jahrhun- dert/-e	*yahr-HOON-dert*
certainly	sicherlich	*ZIKH-er-likh*
chair	(der) Stuhl/ Stühle	*shtool*
chandelier	(der) Kron- leuchter/–	*KROHN-loy'kh-ter*
change	(der) Wechsel/–	*VEX-el*
change (money)	(das) Wechselgeld	*VEX-el-ghelt*
(to) change	wechseln	*VEX-eln*
charming	scharmant, -er, -e, -es	*shar-MAHNT*
chauffeur	(der) Fahrer/–	*FAR-er*
cheap	billig, -er, -e, -es	*BILL-ikh*
check (money)	(der) Scheck/-s	*shek*
(baggage) check	(der) Gepäck- schein/-e	*gheh-PAYK-shine*

checkroom	(die) Garde-robe/-n	*gar-deh-RO-beh*
cheese	(der) Käse	*KAYZ-eh*
chest	(die) Brust/Brüste	*broost*
chicken	(das) Hühn-chen/–	*HŮN-khen*
child	(das) Kind/-er	*kint*
China	(das) China	*KHEE-nah*
Chinese	chinesisch, -er, -e, -es	*khee-NAY-zish*
Chinese (person)	(der) Chi-nese/-n	*khee-NAY-zeh*
	(die) Chine-sin/-nen	*khee-NAY-zin*
chocolate	(die) Schoko-lade	*sho-ko-LA-deh*
church	(die) Kirche/-en	*KEER-kheh*
cigar	(die) Zi-garre/-n	*ts'ee-GAR-eh*
cigarette	(die) Zi-garette/n	*ts'ee-gar-ET-eh*
city	(die) Stadt/Städte	*shtaht*
clean	rein, -er, -e, -es	*rine*
(to) clean	reinigen	*RYE-nee-ghen*
clear	klar, -er, -e, -es	*klahr*
clever	gescheit, -er, -e, -es	*gheh-SHITE*
clock	(die) Uhr/-en	*oor*

close (near)	nahe	*NA-eh*
(to) close	schließen	*SHLEESS'en*
closed	geschlossen	*gheh-SHLOSS'en*
clothes	(die) Kleider	*KLY-der*
coast	(die) Küste/-n	*KÜ-ste*
coat (suit)	(der) Kittel/–	*KIT-el*
(overcoat)	(der) Mantel/ Mäntel	*MAHN-tel*
coffee	(der) Kaffee	*KA-fay*
cold (sickness)	(die) Erkält- ung/-en	*air-KELT-oong*
cold	kalt, -er, -e, -es	*kahlt*
colonel	(der) Oberst/-e	*OH-berst*
color	(die) Farbe/-n	*FAR-beh*
(to) come	kommen	*KOHM'en*
I come	ich komme	*KOHM-eh*
he (she, it) comes	er (sie, es) kommt	*kohmt*
you (we, they) come	Sie (wir, sie) kommen	*KOHM'en*
Come (here)!	Kommen Sie (her)!	*KOHM'en zee (hair)!*
Come in!	Kommen Sie herein!	*KOHM'en zee hair- INE!*
(to) come back	*zurück*kommen (SP)	*ts'oo-RÜK-kohm'en*
comb	(der) Kamm/ Kämme	*kahm*
company (busi- ness)	(die) Gesell- schaft/-en	*gheh-ZELL-shahft*

competition	(die) Konkur-renz	*kohn-koor-ENTS*
complete	vollständig, -er, -e, -es	*FOHL-shtend-ikh*
computer	(der) com-puter/–	*kohm-POO-ter*
concert	(das) Kon-zert/-e	*kon-TS'AIRT*
(to) congratulate	gratulieren	*gra-too-LEER'en*
contract	(der) Vertrag/ Verträge	*fair-TRAHK*
conversation	(die) Unter-haltung/-en	*oon-ter-HAHLT-oong*
cook	(der) Koch/ Köche	*kohkh*
(to) cook	kochen	*KO-khen*
cool	kühl, -er, -e, -es	*kůl*
copy	(die) Kopie/-n	*ko-PEE*
corner	(die) Ecke/-n	*EK-eh*
correct	richtig, -er, -e, -es	*RIKH-tikh*
(to) cost	kosten	*KOHST'en*
cotton	(die) Baum-wolle/-n	*B'OWM-vohl-eh*
cough	(der) Husten	*HOO-sten*
country	(das) Land/ Länder	*lahnt*
cousin	(der) Vetter/-n (die) Kusine/-n	*FET-er* *koo-ZEE-neh*
cow	(die) Kuh/ Kühe	*koo*

crazy	verrückt, -er, -e, -es	*fair-RŮKT*
(to) cross	überqueren	*ů-ber-KVAIR'en*
cup	(die) Tasse/-n	*TAHSS-eh*
customs (office, fee)	(der) Zoll	*ts'ohl*
customs form	(das) Zollformular/-e	*TS'OHL-for-moo-lar*
(to) cut	schneiden	*SHNY-den*
Czech (person)	(der) Tscheche/-n	*CHEH-kheh*
	(die) Tschechin/-nen	*CHEH-khin*
Czechoslovakia	(die) Tschechoslowakei	*cheh-kho-slo-va-KYE*
Czechoslovakian	tschechoslowakisch, -er, -e, -es	*cheh-kho-slo-VA-kish*

D

(to) dance	tanzen	*TAHNTS'en*
dangerous	gefährlich, -er, -e, -es	*gheh-FAIR-likh*
dark	dunkel, dunkler, dunkle, dunkles	*DOONK-el*
date (calendar)	(das) Datum/ Daten	*DA-toom*
date (appointment)	(die) Verabredung/-en	*fair-AHP-ray-doong*

daughter	(die) Tochter/ Töchter	*TOKH-ter*
day	(der) Tag/-e	*tahk*
dead	tot, -er, -e, -es	*toht*
dear	lieb, -er, -e, -es	*leep*
(my) dear	(mein) Liebling	*LEEB-ling*
December	(der) Dezember	*deh-TS'EM-ber*
(to) decide	entscheiden	*ent-SHY-den*
deep	tief, -er, -e, -es	*teef*
delay	(die) Verzöge- rung/-en	*fair-TS'ERG-er- oong*
delighted	sehr erfreut	*zair er-FROYT*
delicious	köstlich, -er, -e, -es	*KERST-likh*
dentist	(der) Zahn- arzt/-ärzte	*TS'AHN-artst*
department store	(das) Waren- haus/-häuser	*VAR-en-howss*
desk	(der) Schreib- tisch/-e	*SHRIPE-tish*
detour	(die) Um- leitung/-en	*OOM-lite-oong*
devil	(der) Teufel/–	*TOY-fel*
dictionary	(das) Wörter- buch/-bücher	*VERT-er-bookh*
different (one)	anderer, an- dere, anderes	*AHN-der-er*
difficult	schwierig, -er, -e, -es	*SHVEE-rikh*
(to) dine	speisen	*SHPY-zen*

dining room	(das) Eßzim-mer/–	*ESS-ts'im-er*
dinner	(das) Abend-essen/–	*AH-bent-ess-en*
direction	(die) Rich-tung/-en	*RIKH-toong*
dirty	schmutzig, -er, -e, -es	*SHMOO-ts'ikh*
disappointed	enttäuscht	*ent-TOYSHT*
discount	(der) Rabatt/-e	*RAHB-aht*
divorced	geschieden	*gheh-SHEED'en*
dizzy	schwindlig, -er, -e, -es	*SHVIND-likh*
(to) do	tun	*toon*

"Do" is not used to ask a question or to form the negative. For a question, simply put the subject after the verb; and for the negative, use **nicht** after the verb.

Do you understand?	Verstehen Sie?	*fair-SHTAY'en zee?*
I don't have	Ich habe nicht	*ikh HA-beh nikht*
Don't go!	Gehen Sie nicht!	*GAY'en zee nikht!*
Don't do that!	Tun Sie das nicht!	*toon zee dahss nikht!*
doctor	(der) Arzt/Ärzte	*artst*
dog	(der) Hund/-e	*hoont*
dollar	(der) Dollar/-s	*DOH-lar*
door	(die) Tür/-en	*tür*
(already) done	(schon) ge-macht	*(shohn) gheh-MAKHT*

donkey	(der) Esel/–	*AYZ-el*
down (direction)	herunter	*hair-OONT-er*
down (location)	unten	*OON-ten*
dress	(das) Kleid/-er	*klite*
(to) drink	trinken	*TRINK'en*
(to) drive	fahren	*FAR'en*
driver	(der) Fahrer/–	*FAR-er*
driver's license	(der) Führer-schein/-e	*FÜR-er-shine*
drunk	betrunken	*beh-TROONK'en*
Dutch	holländisch, -er, -e, -es	*HO-lend-ish*
Dutchman	(der) Holländer/–	*HO-lend-er*
Dutch woman	(die) Holländerin/-nen	*HO-lend-er-in*

E

each	jeder, jede, jedes	*YEH-der*
ear	(das) Ohr/-en	*ohr*
early	früh, -er, -e, -es	*frü*
(to) earn	verdienen	*fair-DEEN'en*
earth	(die) Erde	*AIR-deh*
east	(die) Osten	*OHST-en*
(to) eat	essen	*ESS'en*
egg	(das) Ei/-er	*eye*

eight	acht	*ahkht*
eighteen	achtzehn	*AHKH-ts'ayn*
eighty	achtzig	*AHKH-ts'ikh*
either . . . or	entweder . . . oder	*ent-VAY-der . . . O-der*
electric	elektrisch	*el-EKT-rish*
elephant	(der) Elefant/-en	*el-ef-AHNT*
elevator	(der) Aufzug/ Aufzüge	*OWF-ts'ook*
eleven	elf	*elf*
else (more)	noch	*nokh*
(or) **else**	sonst	*zonst*
embassy	(die) Bot-schaft/-en	*BOAT-shahft*
emergency	(die) Not-lage/-n	*NOHT-la-gheh*
employee	(der, die) An-gestellte/-n	*AHN-gheh-shtel-teh*
employer	(der) Arbeit-geber/–	*AR-bite-gay-ber*
end	(das) Ende/-n	*EN-de*
(to) end	enden	*END'en*
England	(das) England	*ENG-lahnt*
English	englisch, -er, -e, -es	*ENG-lish*
Englishman	(der) Englän-der/–	*ENG-len-der*
Englishwoman	(die) Englän-derin/-nen	*ENG-len-der-in*

entertaining	unterhaltend, -er, -e, -es	*oon-ter-HAHLT-ent*
error	(der) Fehler/–	*FAIL-er*
especially	besonders	*beh-ZOHND-ers*
European	europäisch, -er, -e, -es	*eh-oo-ro-PAY-ish*
European (person)	(der) Europäer/–	*eh-oo-ro-PAY-er*
	(die) Europäerin/-nen	*eh-oo-ro-PAY-er-in*
evening	(der) Abend/-e	*AH-bent*
ever (sometimes)	manchmal	*MAHNKH-mahl*
every	jeder, jede, jedes	*YEH-der*
everybody	alle	*AH-le*
everything	alles	*AH-less*
exact	genau, -er, -e, -es	*gheh-NOW*
excellent	ausgezeichnet, -er, -e, -es	*OWSS-gheh-ts'ykh-net*
except	außer	*OW-ser*
(to) exchange	*um*wechseln (SP)	*OOM-vex-eln*
Excuse me!	Entschuldigung!	*ent-SHOOL-dee-goong*
exit	(der) Ausgang/Ausgänge	*OWSS-gahng*
expensive	teuer, -er, -e, -es	*TOY-er*

experience	(die) Erfah-rung/-en	*air-FAR-oong*
explanation	(die) Erklär-ung/-en	*air-KLAIR-oong*
(to) export	exportieren	*ex-por-TEER'en*
extra	extra	*EX-tra*
eye	(das) Auge/-n	*OW-gheh*

F

face	(das) Ge-sicht/-er	*gheh-ZIKHT*
factory	(die) Fa-brik/-en	*fa-BREEK*
fair (village)	(der) Jahr-markt/-märkte	*YAR-markt*
fall (autumn)	(der) Herbst	*hairpst*
fall (drop)	(der) Sturz/Stürze	*shtoorts*
(to) fall	fallen	*FAHL'en*
family	(die) Fami-lie/-n	*fa-MEE-lee-yeh*
famous	berühmt, -er, -e, -es	*beh-RŮMT*
far	weit	*vite*
How far?	Wie weit?	*vee vite?*
farm	der) Bauern-hof/-höfe	*B'OW-ern-hohf*
farther	weiter	*VITE-er*

fast	schnell, -er, -e, -es	*shnel*
fat	dick, -er, -e, -es	*dick*
father	(der) Vater/Väter	*FA-ter*
February	(der) Februar	*FAY-broo-ar*
(to) feel	fühlen	*FÜ-len*
fever	(das) Fieber/–	*FEE-ber*
few	wenig	*VAY-nikh*
fifteen	fünfzehn	*FÜNF-ts'ayn*
fifty	fünfzig	*FÜNF-ts'ikh*
(to) fight	kämpfen	*KEMP-fen*
(to) fill	füllen	*FÜL'en*
film	(der) Film/-e	*feelm*
finally	endlich	*END-likh*
(to) find	finden	*FIN-den*
(to) find out	*heraus*finden (SP)	*hair-OWSS-fin-den*
finger	(der) Finger/–	*FING-er*
(to) finish	beenden	*beh-END'en*
fire	(das) Feuer/–	*FOY-er*
first	erst, -er, -e, -es	*airst*
(to) fish	fischen	*FISH'en*
five	fünf	*fünf*
flight	(der) Flug/ Flüge	*flook*
floor (of building)	(der) Stock/ Stöcke	*shtohk*
flower	(die) Blume/-n	*BLOOM-eh*

(to) fly	fliegen	*FLEEG'en*
fly (insect)	(die) Fliege/-n	*FLEE-gheh*
food	(das) Essen	*ESS-en*
foot	(der) Fuß/ Füße	*fooss*
for	für	*für*
foreigner	(der) Aus- länder/–	*OWSS-lend-er*
	(die) Auslän- derin/-nen	*OWSS-lend-er-in*
(to) forget	vergessen	*fair-GUESS'en*
Don't forget!	Nicht vergessen!	*nikht fair- GUESS'en!*
fork	(die) Gabel/-n	*GA-bel*
forty	vierzig	*FEER-ts'ikh*
fountain	(der) Springbrun- nen/–	*SHPRING-broon- en*
four	vier	*feer*
fourteen	vierzehn	*FEER-ts'ayn*
fox	(der) Fuchs/ Füchse	*foox*
France	(das) Frank- reich	*FRAHNK-ry'kh*
free	frei, -er, -e, -es	*fry*
French	französisch, -er, -e, -es	*frahn-TS'ER-zish*
Frenchman	(der) Franzo- ze/-n	*frahn-TS'OH-zeh*
Frenchwoman	(die) Franzö- sin/-nen	*frahn-TS'ER-zin*

frequently	oft	*ohft*
fresh	frisch, -er, -e, -es	*frish*
Friday	(der) Freitag/-e	*FRY-tahk*
fried	gebraten, -er, -e, -es	*gheh-BRAHT'en*
friend	(der) Freund/-e	*froynt*
	(die) Freun-din/-nen	*FROYN-din*
from	von	*fohn*
from the	von dem *or* vom (m, n)	*fohn daim, fohm*
	von der (f)	*fohn dair*
	von den (pl)	*fohn dain*
(in) front of	vor	*fohr*
fruit	(die) Frucht/ Früchte	*frookht*
full	voll, -er, -e, -es	*fohl*
funny	komisch, -er, -e, -es	*KOHM-ish*
future	(die) Zukunft	*TS'OO-koonft*

G

game	(das) Spiel/-e	*shpeel*
garden	(der) Garten/Gär-ten	*GAR-ten*
gasoline	(das) Benzin	*ben-TS'EEN*
gas station	(die) Tank-stelle/-n	*TAHNK-shtel-leh*
garage	(die) Garage/-n	*gar-AH-zheh*

general	allgemein, -er, -e, -es	*AHL-gheh-mine*
general (military)	(der) General/ Generäle	*gheh-neh-RAHL*
gentlemen!	(meine) Herrschaften!	*(MINE-eh) HAIR-shahft-en!*
genuine	echt, -er, -e, -es	*ekht*
German	deutsch, -er, -e, -es	*doych*
German (person)	(der, die) Deutsche/-n	*DOYCH-eh*
Germany	(das) Deutschland	*DOYCH-lahnt*
(to) get	bekommen	*beh-KOHM'en*
(to) get off	*aus*steigen (SP)	*OWSS-shty-ghen*
(to) get on (into)	*ein*steigen (SP)	*INE-shty-ghen*
(to) get up	*auf*stehen (SP)	*OWF-shtay'en*
(to) get up (on something)	*auf*steigen (SP)	*OWF-shty-ghen*
Get out!	Raus!	*R'OWSS!*
Give me . . .	Geben Sie mir . . .	*GAY-ben zee meer . . .*
(to) give	geben	*GAY-ben*
girl	(das) Mädchen/–	*MAYT-yen*
glass	(das) Glas/ Gläser	*glahss*

(eye)glasses	(die) Brille/-n	*BRIL-leh*
glove	(der) Hand-schuh/-e	*HAHNT-shoo*
(to) go	gehen	*GAY'en*
I go	ich gehe	*GAY-eh*
he (she, it) goes	er (sie, es) geht	*gait*
you (we, they) go	Sie (wir, sie) gehen	*GAY'en*
(to) go away	*weg*gehen (SP)	*VEK-gay'en*
Go away!	Gehen Sie weg!	*GAY'en zee vek!*
(to) go back	*zurück*gehen (SP)	*ts'oo-RŮK-gay'en*
(to) go on	*weiter*gehen (SP)	*VITE-er-gay'en*
Go on!	Gehen Sie weiter!	*GAY'en zee VITE-er!*
God	(der) Gott/ Götter	*goht*
gold	(das) Gold	*gohlt*
good	gut	*goot*
Good-bye!	Auf Wieder-sehen!	*owf VEE-dair-zay'en*
government	(die) Regier-ung/-en	*reh-GEER-oong*
grandfather	(der) Groß-vater/-väter	*GROHSS-fa-ter*
grandmother	(die) Groß-mutter/-mütter	*GROHSS-moot-er*
grateful	dankbar, -er, -e, -es	*DAHNK-bar*
gray	grau	*gr'ow*

great	groß, -er, -e, -es	*gross*
a great many	sehr viele	*zair FEEL-eh*
Greece	(das) Griechen-land	*GREE-khen-lahnt*
Greek	griechisch, -er, -e, -es	*GREE-khish*
Greek (person)	(der) Grieche/-n	*GREE-kheh*
	(die) Grie-chin/-nen	*GREE-khin*
green	grün, -er, -e, -es	*grün*
gross (weight)	Brutto	*BROOT-toh*
group	(die) Gruppe/-n	*GROOP-eh*
guide	(der) Reise-führer/–	*RY-zeh-fŭr-er*
guitar	(die) Gitarre/-n	*ghee-TAR-eh*

H

hair	(das) Haar/-e	*har*
hairbrush	(die) Haar-bürste/-n	*HAR-bŭr-steh*
haircut	(der) Haar-schnitt/-e	*HAR-shnit*
half	halb, -er, -e, -es	*hahlp*
hand	(die) Hand/Hände	*hahnt*
happy	glücklich, -er, -e, -es	*GLŬK-likh*
hat	(der) Hut/Hüte	*hoot*
(to) have	haben	*HAHB'en*

I have	ich habe	*HAHB-eh*
he (she, it) has	er (sie, es) hat	*haht*
you (we, they) have	Sie (wir, sie) haben	*HAHB'en*
Have you . . . ?	Haben Sie . . . ?	*HAHB-en zee . . . ?*
he	er	*air*
head	(der) Kopf	*kohpf*
heart	(das) Herz/-en	*hair'ts*
heavy	schwer, -er, -e, -es	*shvair*
(to) hear	hören	*HER'en*
Hello! (phone)	Hallo!	*HA-lo!*
(to) help	helfen	*HELF'en*
Help!	Hilfe!	*HEEL-feh!*
her (direct object)	sie	*zee*
(to) her	ihr	*eer*
her (possessive)	ihr (m), ihre (f), ihr (n); ihre (pl)	*eer, EER-eh*
here	hier	*heer*
high	hoch, hoher, hohe, hohes	*hohkh, HO-er*
higher	höher, -er, -e, -es	*HER-er*
highway	(die) Auto- bahn/-en	*OW-toh-bahn*
hill	(der) Hügel/–	*HÜG-el*

him	ihn	*een*
(to) him	ihm	*eem*
his	sein (m), seine (f), sein (n); seine (pl)	*ZINE, ZINE-eh*
history	(die) Ge-schichte/-n	*gheh-SHIKH-teh*
Holland	(das) Holland	*HO-lahnt*
(at) home	zu Hause	*ts'oo HOW-zeh*
horse	(das) Pferd/-e	*pfairt*
hospital	(das) Kranken-haus/-häuser	*KRAHNK-en-howss*
hot	heiß, -er, -e, -es	*hice*
hotel	(das) Hotel/-s	*ho-TEL*
hour	(die) Stunde/-n	*SHTOON-deh*
house	(das) Haus/ Häuser	*howss*
how	wie	*vee*
however	jedoch	*yeh-DOHKH*
hundred	hundert	*HOON-dert*
Hungary	(das) Ungarn	*OON-garn*
Hungarian	ungarisch, -er, -e, -es	*OON-gar-ish*
Hungarian (person)	(der) Ungar/ -en	*OON-gar*
	(die) Ungarin/ -nen	*OON-gar-in*
hungry	hungrig, -er -e, -es	*HOONG-rikh*
(to) hurry	eilen	*EYE-len*

Hurry up!	Beeilen Sie sich!	*beh-EYE-len zee zikh!*
husband	(der) Mann/ Männer	*mahn*

I

I	ich	*ikh*
ice	(das) Eis	*ice*
ice cream	(das) Eis	*ice*
idiot	(der) Idiot/-en	*ee-D'YOHT*
if	wenn	*ven*
imagine	sich *vor*stellen (SP)	*zikh FOR-shtel'en*
Just imagine!	Stellen Sie sich vor!	*SHTEL'en zee zikh for!*
(to) import	importieren	*im-port-EER'en*
important	wichtig, -er, -e, -es	*VIKH-tikh*
impossible	unmöglich, -er, -e, -es	*OON-merg-likh*
in	in	*in*
in the	in dem *or* im (m, n)	*in daem, im*
	in der (f)	*in dair*
	in den (pl)	*in daen*
including	einschließlich	*INE-shlees-likh*
industry	(die) Industrie/-n	*in-doo-STREE*
information	(die) Auskunft	*OWSS-koonft*

inn	(die) Gast- stätte/-n	*GAHST-shtet-eh*
inquiry	(die) Erkundi- gung/-en	*air-KOON-dee-goong*
inside	innen *or* drin	*IN-en, drin*
instead	anstatt	*ahn-SHTAHT*
intelligent	intelligent, -er, -e, -es	*in-tel-ee-GHENT*
interested	interessiert, -er, -e, -es	*in-tair-ess-EERT*
interesting	interessant, -er, -e, -es	*in-tair-ess-AHNT*
interpreter	(der) Dol- metscher/–	*DOHL-meh-cher*
into the	in den (m) in die (f) in das *or* ins (n) in die (pl)	*in daen* *in dee* *in dahss, inss* *in dee*
(to) introduce	*vor*stellen (SP)	*FOR-shtel'en*
May I intro- duce . . .	Darf ich vor- stellen . . .	*darf ikh FOR-shtel'- en . . .*
invitation	(die) Einla- dung/-en	*INE-la-doong*
(he, she, it) is	(er, sie, es) ist	*isst*
there is	es gibt	*ess ghipt*
island	(die) Insel/-n	*IN-zel*
it	es	*ess*
it is	es ist	*ess isst*

its	sein (m), seine (f), sein (n); seine (pl)	*zine, ZINE-eh*
Italian	italienisch, -er, -e, -es	*ee-tahl-YEH-nish*
Italian (person)	(der) Italie-ner/–	*ee-tahl-YEH-ner*
	(die) Italiener-in/-nen	*ee-tahl-YEH-ner-in*
Italy	(das) Italien	*ee-TA-lee-yen*

J

jacket	(die) Jacke/-n	*YA-keh*
January	(der) Januar	*YA-noo-ar*
Japan	(das) Japan	*YA-pahn*
Japanese	japanisch, -er, -e, es	*ya-PAHN-ish*
Japanese (person)	(der) Ja-paner/–	*ya-PAHN-er*
	(die) Japaner-in/-nen	*ya-PAHN-er-in*
jewelry	(der) Schmuck	*shmook*
Jewish	jüdisch, -er, -e, -es	*YŮ-dish*
job	(die) Arbeit/-en	*AR-bite*
joke	(der) Witz/-e	*vitz*
(to) joke	scherzen	*SHAIR-ts'en*
July	(der) Juli	*YOO-lee*
June	(der) Juni	*YOO-nee*

| just (only) | nur | *noor* |
| just (now) | eben | *AY-ben* |

K

(to) keep	behalten	*beh-HAHLT'en*
Keep out!	Eintritt ver- boten!	*INE-trit fair-BO-ten!*
key	(der) Schlüs- sel/–	*SHLÜS-sel*
kind	liebenswürdig, -er, -e, -es	*LEE-benss-vür-dikh*
king	(der) König/-e	*KERN-ig*
kiss	(der) Kuß/ Küße	*kooss*
kitchen	(die) Küche/-n	*KÜ-kheh*
knee	(das) Knie/–	*k'nee*
knife	(das) Messer/–	*MESS-er*
(to) know (a fact)	wissen	*VISS'en*
(to know (to be acquainted with)	kennen	*KEN'en*
(to) know how	können	*KERN'en*
Do you know . . . ?	Wissen Sie . . . ?	*VISS'en zee?*
Who knows?	Wer weiß?	*vair vice?*

L

ladies' room	(die) Damen-toilette/-en	*DA-men-twa-let-eh*
ladies and gentlemen!	Meine Damen und Herren!	*MINE-eh DAHM-en oont hair'n!*
lady	(die) Dame/-n	*DAH-meh*
lake	(der) See/-n	*zay*
lamb	(das) Lamm/ Lämmer	*lahm*
land	(das) Land/ Länder	*lahnt*
language	(die) Sprache/-n	*SPRAH-kheh*
large	groß, -er, -e, -es	*grohss*
larger	größer, -er, -e, -es	*GRERSS-er*
last	letzt, -er, -e, -es	*LETST*
late	spät, -er, -e, -es	*shpayt*
later	später	*SHPAYT-er*
lawyer	(der) Rechtsan-walt/-an-wälte	*REKHTS-ahn-vahlt*
(to) learn	lernen	*LAIRN'en*
leather	(das) Leder	*LAID-er*
(to) leave	verlassen	*fair-LAHSS'en*
left (direction)	links	*links*
leg	(das) Bein/-e	*bine*

lemon	(die) Zi-trone/-n	ts'it-RO-ne
(to) lend	verleihen	fair-LY-en
less	weniger	VAY-nig-er
lesson	(die) Stunde/-n	SHTOON-deh
(to) let (permit)	lassen	LAHSS'en
Let us . . .	Lassen Sie uns . . .	LAHSS'en zee oonss . . .
Let's go!	Gehen wir!	GAY'en veer!
letter (mail)	(der) Brief/-e	breef
lettuce	(der) Kopfsa-lat	KOHPF-za-laht
liberty	(die) Freiheit/-en	FRY-hite
lieutenant	(der) Leut-nant/-s	LOYT-nahnt
life	(das) Leben	LAYB-en
(to) lift	*auf*heben (SP)	OWF-hayb'en
light (weight)	leicht, -er, -e, -es	ly'kht
light (illumina-tion)	(das) Licht/-er	likht
like	wie	vee
Like this.	Wie das.	vee dahss.
(to) like	gerne haben	GAIR-neh HAHB'en
lion	(der) Löwe/-n	LERV-eh
lip	(die) Lippe/-n	LIP-eh
list	(die) Liste/-n	LIST-eh
(to) listen	*zu*hören (SP)	TS'OO-her'en

little (small)	klein, -er, -e, -es	*kline*
a little	ein bißchen	*ine BISS-yen*
(to) live	leben	*LAYB'en*
living room	(das) Wohn-zimmer/–	*VOHN-ts'im-er*
long	lang, -er, -e, -es	*lahng*
(to) look	schauen	*SH'OW'en*
Look out!	Gib acht!	*ghip ahkht!*
(to) lose	verlieren	*fair-LEER'en*
lost	verloren	*fair-LOHR'en*
lost and found office	(das) Fund-büro/-s	*FOONT-bŭ-ro*
(a) lot	viel	*feel*
(to) love	lieben	*LEE-ben*
low	niedrig, -er, -e, -es	*NEED-rikh*
luck	(das) Glück	*glŭk*
Good luck!	Viel Glück!	*feel glŭk*
bad luck	(das) Pech	*pekh*
luggage	(das) Gepäck	*gheh-PAYK*
lunch	(das) Mittag-essen/–	*MIT-tahk-ess-en*

M

| machine | (die) Ma-schine/-n | *mah-SHEE-neh* |

madam	gnädige Frau	*GNAY-dee-gheh FR'OW*
made	gemacht, -er, -e, -es	*gheh-MAKHT*
maid (servant)	(das) Dienst- mädchen/–	*DEENST-mayt-yen*
mailbox	(der) Brief- kasten/–	*BREEF-kahst-en*
(to) make	machen	*MAKH'en*
man	(der) Mann/ Männer	*mahn*
manager	(der) Verwal- ter/-wälter	*fair-VAHL-ter*
many	viele	*FEEL-eh*
map	(die) Karte/-n	*KAR-teh*
March	(der) März	*mairts*
market	(der) Markt/ Märkte	*markt*
married	veheiratet	*fair-HI-raht-et*
mass (religious)	(die) Messe/-n	*MESS-eh*
match (for fire)	(das) Streich- holz/-hölzer	*SHTRY'KH-hohlts*
(What's the) matter?	Was ist los?	*vahss isst lohss?*
May I?	Darf ich?	*darf ikh?*
May	(der) Mai	*my*
maybe	vielleicht	*feel-LY'KHT*
me	mich	*mikh*
(to) me	mir	*meer*
(to) mean	meinen	*MINE-en*

meat	(das) Fleisch	*fly'sh*
mechanic	(der) Mecha-niker/–	*meh-KHAHN-ik-er*
medicine	(die) Medizin/-en	*meh-dee-TS'EEN*
Mediterranean	(das) Mittel-meer	*MIT-el-mair*
(to) meet	treffen	*TREF'en*
meeting	(das) Zusamen-treffen/–	*ts'oo-ZAHM-en-tref'en*
member	(das) Mit-glied/-er	*MIT-gleet*
(to) mend	reparieren	*ray-par-EER'en*
men	(die) Männer	*MEN-er*
men's room	(die) Herren-toilette/-n	*HAIR-en-twa-let-eh*
menu	(die) Speise-karte/-n	*SHPY-zeh-kar-teh*
message	(die) Mitteil-ung/-en	*MIT-tile-oong*
Mexican	mexikanisch, -er, -e, -es	*mex-ih-KA-nish*
Mexican (person)	(der) Mexika-ner/–	*mex-ih-KA-ner*
	(die) Mexika-nerin/-nen	*Mex-ih-KA-ner-in*
middle	(die) Mitte/-n	*MIT-eh*
in the middle	mitten drin	*MIT-en drin*
middle (adj)	mittler, -er, -e, -es	*MIT-ler*
mile	(die) Meile/-n	*MILE-eh*

milk	(die) Milch	*meelkh*
million	(die) Million/-en	*MEEL-yohn*
minister (clergy)	(der) Geistliche	*GHY'ST-lee-kheh*
minute	(die) Minute/-n	*mee-NOO-teh*
Miss	(das) Fräu-lein/–	*FROY-line*
(to) miss (emotion)	vermissen	*fair-MISS'en*
(to) miss (a train, etc.)	verpassen	*fair-PAHSS'en*
mistake	(der) Fehler/–	*FAY-ler*
misunderstanding	(das) Mißver-ständnis/-se	*MISS-fair-shtend-niss*
Mr.	Herr/-en	*hair*
Mrs.	Frau	*fr'ow*
model	(das) Modell/-e	*MO-del*
modern	modern, -er, -e, -es	*mo-DAIRN*
moment	(der) Mo-ment/-en	*mo-MENT*
Monday	(der) Montag/-e	*MOHN-tahk*
money	(das) Geld	*ghelt*
monkey	(der) Affe/-n	*AHF-eh*
month	(der) Monat/-e	*MO-naht*
monument	(das) Denk-mal/-mäler	*DENK-mahl*
moon	(der) Mond	*mohnt*
more	mehr	*mair*

morning	(der) Mor-gen/–	*MORE-ghen*
mostly	meistens	*MY-stens*
mother	(die) Mutter/ Mütter	*MOOT-ter*
mother-in-law	(die) Schwie-germutter/ -mütter	*SHVEE-gher-moot-ter*
motor	(der) Motor/ -en	*MO-tohr*
motorcycle	(das) Motor-rad/-räder	*MO-tohr-raht*
mountain	(der) Berg/-e	*bairk*
mouth	(der) Mund/ Münder	*moont*
mouse	(die) Maus/ Mäuse	*m'owss*
movies	(das) Kino/-s	*KEE-no*
much	viel	*feel*
museum	(das) Muse-um/Museen	*moo-ZAY-oom*
music	(die) Musik	*moo-ZEEK*
musician	(der) Musi-ker/–	*MOO-zee-ker*
must	müssen	*MÜSS'en*
I must go.	Ich muß gehen.	*ikh mooss GAY'en.*
mustache	(der) Schnurr-bart/-bärte	*SHNOOR-bart*
mustard	(der) Senf	*zenf*

| my | mein (m), meine (f), mein (n); meine (pl) | *mine, MINE-eh* |

N

name	(der) Name/-n	*NA-meh*
napkin	(die) Serviette/-n	*zairv-YET-eh*
narrow	eng, -er, -e, -es,	*ehng*
navy	(die) Marine/-n	*ma-REE-neh*
near	nahe, -er, -e, -es,	*NA-eh*
necessary	notwendig, -er, -e, es	*NOHT-ven-dikh*
neck	(der) Nacken/–	*NAHK-en*
necktie	(die) Krawatte/-n	*kra-VAHT-eh*
(to) need	brauchen	*BROW-khen*
neighborhood	(die) Nachbarschaft/-en	*NAHKH-bar-shahft*
nephew	(der) Neffe/-n	*NEF-eh*
nervous	nervös, -er, -e, -es	*nair-VERSS*
net profit	(der) Reingewinn/-e	*RINE-gheh-vin*
net (weight)	netto	*NET-toh*
never	niemals	*NEE-mahls*

Never mind!	Das macht nichts!	*dahss makht nikhts!*
new	neu, -er, -e, -es	*noy*
news	(die) Nach-richt/-en	*NAHKH-rikht*
newspaper	(die) Zeitung/-en	*TS'Y-toong*
next	nächst, -er, -e, -es,	*nayxt*
nice	nett, -er, -e, -es,	*net*
night	(die) Nacht/Nächte	*nahkht*
nightclub	(das) Nacht-lokal/-en	*NAHKHT-lo-kahl*
nightgown	(das) Nacht-hemd/-e	*NAHKHT-hemt*
nine	neun	*noyn*
nineteen	neunzehn	*NOYN-ts'ayn*
ninety	neunzig	*NOYN-ts'ikh*
no	nein	*nine*
no (not a)	kein (m), keine (f), kein (n); keine (pl)	*kine, KY-neh*
nobody	niemand	*NEE-mahnt*
noise	(der) Lärm	*lairm*
none	keine	*KY-neh*
noon	(der) Mittag/-e	*MIT-tahk*
north	(der) Norden	*NOR-den*
nose	(die) Nase/-n	*NA-zeh*

not	nicht	*nikht*
not any	kein, keine, kein	*kine, KY-neh*
not yet	noch nicht	*nohkh nikht*
nothing	nichts	*nikhts*
nothing at all	garnichts	*GAR-nikhts*
November	(der) November	*no-VEM-ber*
now	jetzt	*yetst*
nowhere	nirgends	*NEER-ghents*
number	(die) Nummer/–	*NOOM-er*

O

occasionally	dann und wann	*dahn oont vahn*
occupied	besetzt, -er, -e, -es	*beh-ZETST*
ocean	(der) Ozean/-e	*OH-ts'eh-ahn*
October	(der) Oktober	*ok-TOH-ber*
of	von	*fohn*
of the	des (m, n), der (f); der (pl)	*dess* *dair* *dair*
off	ab	*ahp*
(to) offer	*an*bieten (SP)	*AHN-beet'en*
office	(das) Büro/-s	*BÜ-ro*
officer	(der) Offizier/-e	*off-fee-TS'EER*

official	(der) Beamte/-n	*beh-AHM-teh*
often	oft	*ohft*
oil	(das) Öl	*erl*
okay	alles in Ordnung	*AH-less in ORD-noong*
old	alt, -er, -e, -es,	*ahlt*
on	auf	*ow'f*
on the	auf dem (m, n)	*owf daim*
	auf der (f)	*owf dair*
	auf den (pl)	*owf dain*
on time	pünktlich, -er, -e, -es	*PÜNKT-likh*
once	einst	*ine'st*
At once!	Sofort!	*zo-FORT!*
one	ein, -er, -e,	*ine*
only	nur	*noor*
onto the	auf den (m)	*owf dain*
	auf die (f)	*owf dee*
	auf das *or* aufs (n)	*owf dahss, owfs*
	auf die (pl)	*owf dee*
open	offen, -er, -e, -es	*OHF'en*
(to) open	öffnen	*ERF-nen*
opera	(die) Oper/-n	*OH-per*
opinion	(die) Meinung/-en	*MINE-oong*
opportunity	(die) Gelegenheit/-en	*gheh-LAIG-en-hite*
opposite	gegenüber	*gheh-gheh-NÜ-ber*

or	oder	*OH-der*
orange	(die) Apfel-sine/-n	*ahp-fel-ZEF-neh*
orchestra	(das) Orche-ster/–	*or-KEH-ster*
order	(der) Befehl/-e	*beh-FAIL*
(to) order	bestellen	*beh-SHTEL'en*
in order to	um . . . zu	*oom . . . ts'oo*
original	ursprünglich, -er, -e, -es,	*OOR-shprüng-likh*
other	anderer, andere, anderes	*AHN-der-er*
ought	sollen	*ZOHL'en*
You ought to . . .	Sie sollten . . .	*zee ZOHLT'en*
our	unser (m), unsere (f), unser (n); unsere (pl)	*OON-zer OON-ser-eh*
outside	draußen	*DR'OW-sen*
over	über	*Ü-ber*
(to) owe	schulden	*SHOOL-den*
(to) own	besitzen	*beh-ZITS'en*
owner	(der) Besit-zer/–	*beh-ZIT-ser*
ox	(der) Ochse/-n	*ohx*

P

package	(das) Paket/-te	*pa-KAYT*
paid	bezahlt	*beh-TS'AHLT*
pain	(der) Schmerz/-en	*shmairts*
(to) paint	malen	*MAHL-en*
painting	(das) Gemäl-de/–	*gheh-MAYL-deh*
palace	(das) Schloß/Schlösser	*shlohss*
pants	(die) Hose/-n	*HO-zeh*
paper	(das) Papier/-e	*pa-PEER*
parade	(die) Pa-rade/-n	*pa-RAHD-eh*
Pardon me!	Entschuldigen Sie!	*ent-SHOOL-dig'en zee!*
(to) park	parken	*PARK'en*
park	(der) Park	*park*
parents	(die) Eltern	*EL-tern*
part	(der) Teil/-e	*tile*
partner (business)	(der) Teil-haber/–	*TILE-hahb-er*
passenger	(der) Fahr-gast/-gäste	*FAR-gahst*
passport	(der) Pass/Pässe	*pahss*
past	(die) Vergan-genheit	*fair-GAHNG-en-hite*

(to) pay	zahlen	*TS'AHL'en*
peace	(der) Frieden	*FREE-den*
pen	(die) Schreib-feder/–	*SHRIPE-fay-der*
pencil	(der) Blei-stift/-e	*BLY-shtift*
people	(die) Leute	*LOY-teh*
percent	(das) Prozent	*pro-TS'ENT*
perfect	vollkommen, -er, -e, es	*fohl-KOHM'en*
perfume	(das) Par-füm/-e	*par-FŮM*
perhaps	vielleicht	*feel-LY'KHT*
permitted	erlaubt, -er, -e, -es	*air-L'OWPT*
person	(die) Person/-en	*per-ZOHN*
photo	(das) Foto/-s	*FO-toh*
piano	(das) Kla-vier/-e	*klah-VEER*
picture	(das) Bild/-er	*bilt*
piece	(das) Stück/-e	*stŮk*
pier	(der) Pier/-s	*peer*
pill	(die) Pille/-n	*PIL-eh*
pillow	(das) Kissen/–	*KISS'en*
pin	(die) Steck-nadel/–	*SHTEK-nahd-el*
pink	rosa	*RO-za*
pipe (smoking)	(die) Pfeife/-n	*P'FY-feh*

place	(der) Platz/ Plätze	*plahts*
plan	(der) Plan/ Pläne	*plahn*
plane (airplane)	(das) Flug- zeug/-e	*FLOOK-ts'oyk*
planet	(der) Planet/ -en	*pla-NEHT*
plant (garden)	(die) Pflanze/ -n	*P'FLAHN-ts'eh*
plant (factory)	(die) Fabrik- anlage/-n	*fa-BRICK-ahn-la- gheh*
plate	(der) Teller/–	*TEL-er*
(to) play	spielen	*SHPEEL'en*
pleasant	angenehm, -er, -e, -es	*AHN-gheh-naym*
Please!	Bitte!	*BIT-teh*
pleasure	(das) Vergnü- gen/–	*fairg-NŮG-en*
pocket	(die) Tasche/-n	*TA-sheh*
poem	(das) Ge- dicht/-e	*gheh-DIKHT*
(to) point out	zeigen	*TS'Y-ghen*
Poland	(das) Polen	*PO-len*
Pole (person)	(der) Pole/-n (die) Polin/ -nen	*PO-leh* *PO-lin*
policeman	(der) Polizist/ -en	*po-leets-ISST*
police station	(die) Polizei- wache	*po-leets-EYE-va-kheh*

Polish	polnisch, -er, -e, -es	*POHL-nish*
polite	höflich -er, -e, -es,	*HERF-likh*
poor	arm, -er, -e, -es,	*arm*
pope	(der) Papst/ Päpste	*pahpst*
popular	beliebt, -er	*beh-LEEPT*
pork	(das) Schweine- fleisch	*SHVY-ne-fly'sh*
Portugal	(das) Portugal	*PORT-oo-gahl*
possible	möglich, -er, -e, -es	*MERG-likh*
postcard	(die) Post- karte/-n	*POHST-kar-teh*
post office	(das) Postamt/ -ämter	*POHST-ahmt*
potato	(die) Kar- toffel/-n	*kar-TOFF-el*
pound (weight)	(das) Pfund/-e	*pfoont*
(to) practice	üben	*Ü-ben*
(to) prefer	*vor*ziehen (SP)	*FOR-ts'ee'en*
pregnant	schwanger, -er, -e, -es	*SHVAHNG-er*
(to) prepare	*vor*bereiten (SP)	*FOR-beh-rite'en*
present (gift)	(das) Ge- schenk/-e	*gheh-SHENK*
president	(der) Präsi- dent/-en	*preh-zee-DENT*

(to) press (clothes)	bügeln	*BÜG-eln*
pretty	hübsch, -er, -e, -es	*hüpsh*
previously	vorher	*FOR-hair*
price	(der) Preis/-e	*price*
priest	(der) Priester/–	*PREE-ster*
prince	(der) Prinz/-e	*prints*
princess	(die) Prinzessin/-nen	*prints-ESS-in*
prison	(das) Gefängnis/-se	*gheh-FENG-niss*
private	privat, -er, -e, -es	*pree-VAHT*
probable	wahrscheinlich, -er, -e, -es	*VAR-shine-likh*
problem	(das) Problem/-e	*pro-BLAYM*
production	(die) Produktion	*pro-dook-TS'YOHN*
profession	(der) Beruf/-e	*beh-ROOF*
profits	(der) Profit	*pro-FEET*
professor	(der) Professor/-en	*pro-FESS-or*
program	(das) Programm/-e	*pro-GRAHM*
(to) promise	versprechen	*fair-SHPREKH'en*
(to) pronounce	*aus*sprechen (SP)	*OWSS-shprekh'en*
propaganda	(die) Propaganda	*pro-pa-GAHN-da*

property	(das) Eigentum	*EYE-ghen-toom*
Protestant	(der) Prote- stant/-en	*pro-test-AHNT*
public	öffentlich, -er, -e, -es	*ERF-ent-likh*
publicity	(die) Öffent- lichkeit	*ERF-ent-likh-kite*
publisher	(der) Ver- leger/–	*fair-LAIG-er*
(to) pull	ziehen	*TS'EE'en*
(to) purchase	kaufen	*KOWF'en*
purple	purpurfarben	*poor-POOR-far-ben*
purse	(der) Geld- beutel/–	*GHELT-boy-tel*
(to) push	schieben	*SHEEB'en*
(to) put down	*hin*legen (SP)	*HIN-layg'en*
(to) put on	*an*legen (SP)	*AHN-layg'en*

Q

quality	(die) Quali- tät/-en	*kva-lee-TAIT*
queen	(die) Köni- gin/-nen	*KERN-ig-in*
question	(die) Frage/-n	*FRA-gheh*
quick	schnell, -er, -e, -es,	*shnel*
quiet	still, -er, -e, -es,	*shteel*
quite	ganz	*gahnts*

R

Rabbi	(der) Rabbi-ner/–	*ra-BIN-er*
rabbit	(das) Kanin-chen/–	*kahn-EEN-khen*
race (contest)	(das) Wettren-nen/–	*VET-ren'en*
radio	(das) Radio/-s	*RA-dee-o*
railroad	(die) Eisen-bahn/-en	*EYE-zen-bahn*
(to) rain	regnen	*RAYG'nen*
It's raining!	Es regnet!	*ess RAYG-net!*
raincoat	(der) Regen-mantel/-mäntel	*RAY-ghen-mahn-tel*
rarely	selten	*ZEL-ten*
rate (of exchange)	(der) Kurs	*koorss*
razor	(der) Rasierap-parat/-e	*ra-ZEER-ahp-par-aht*
(to) read	lesen	*LAYZ'en*
ready (finished)	fertig, -er, -e, -es	*FAIR-tikh*
real	wirklich, -er, -e, -es	*VEER-klikh*
receipt	(die) Quit-tung/-en	*KVIT-toong*
(to) receive	erhalten	*air-HAHLT'en*
recent	kürzlich, -er, -e, -es	*KÜRTS-likh*

(to) recognize	erkennen	*air-KEN'en*
(to) recommend	empfehlen	*emp-FAIL'en*
red	rot, -er, -e, -es,	*roht*
refrigerator	(der) Kühl- schrank/ -schränke	*KŮL-shrahnk*
(to) refuse	*ab*schlagen (SP)	*AHP-shlag'en*
(My) regards to . . .	Meine Grüße an . . .	*MINE-eh GRŮ-seh ahn . . .*
regular	regelrecht, -er, -e, -es,	*RAY-ghel-rekht*
religion	(die) Reli- gion/-en	*reh-lee-G'YOHN*
(to) remain	bleiben	*BLY-ben*
(to) remember	sich erinnern	*zikh eh-RIN-ern*
(to) rent	mieten	*MEET'en*
(to) repair	reparieren	*reh-par-EER'en*
(to) repeat	wiederholen	*vee-der-HO-len*
report	(der) Bericht/-e	*beh-RIKHT*
(to) represent	repräsentieren	*reh-pray-ZEN- TEER'en*
representative	(der) Vertre- ter/–	*fair-TRAY-ter*
responsible	verantwort- lich, -er, -e, -es	*fair-AHNT-vort-likh*
(the) rest	(das) Übrige	*ŮB-rig-eh*
(to) rest	sich *aus*ruhen (SP)	*zikh OW'SS-roo'en*
restaurant	(das) Restau- rant/-s	*res-toh-RAHNG*

(to) return	*zurück*kehren (SP)	*ts'oo-RŮK-kair'en*
revolution	(die) Revolution/-en	*reh-vo-loo-TS'YOHN*
reward	(die) Belohnung/-en	*beh-LO-noong*
rich	reich, -er, -e, -es	*ry'kh*
(to) ride (a horse)	reiten	*RY-ten*
(to) ride (in a vehicle)	fahren (mit)	*FAR'en*
right (not left)	rechts	*rekhts*
right (correct)	richtig, -er, -e, -es	*RIKH-tikh*
Right away!	Sofort!	*zo-FORT!*
ring	(der) Ring/-e	*ring*
riot	(der) Aufruhr/-en	*OWF-roor*
river	(der) Fluß/ Flüsse	*flooss*
road	(der) Weg/-e	*vek*
roof	(das) Dach/ Dächer	*dakh*
room	(das) Zimmer/–	*TS'IM-er*
room service	(die) Zimmerbedienung	*TS'IM-er-beh-dee-noong*
round trip	(die) Rundfahrt/-en	*ROONT-fahrt*
route	(der) Weg/-e	*vek*

rug	(der) Tep- pich/-e	*TEP-ikh*
(to) run	laufen	*L'OW-fen*
Russia	(das) Ruß- land	*ROOSS-lahnt*
Russian	russisch, -er, -e, -es	*ROOSS-ish*
Russian (person)	(der) Russe/-n (die) Russin/- nen	*ROOSS-eh* *ROOSS-in*

S

sad	traurig, -er, -e, -es	*TR'OW-rikh*
safe	sicher, -er, -e, -es	*ZIK-kher*
said	gesagt	*gheh-ZAKT*
sailor	(der) See- mann/ -leute	*(der) ZAY-mahn*
saint	(der, die) Heilige	*HI-lee-gheh*
salad	(der) Salat	*za-LAHT*
salary	(das) Gehalt/ Gehälter	*gheh-HAHLT*
sale	(der) Ver- kauf/Ver- käufe	*fair-KOWF*
same	derselbe, diesel- be, dasselbe	*dair-ZEL-beh, dee- ZEL-beh, dahss- ZEL-beh*

sandwich	(das) belegte Butterbrot	*beh-LAKE-teh boot-er-BROHT*
Saturday	(der) Sams-tag/-e	*ZAHMSS-tahk*
(to) say	sagen	*ZAHG'en*
school	(die) Schule/-n	*SHOOL-eh*
scissors	(die) Schere/-n	*SHAIR-eh*
Scottish	schottisch, -er, -e, -es	*SHOHT-tish*
Scotsman	(der) Schot-te/-n	*SHOHT-teh*
Scotswoman	(die) Schottin/-nen	*SHOHT-tin*
Scotland	Schottland	*SHOHT-lahnt*
sea	(das) Meer/-e	*mair*
season	(die) Jahres-zeit/-en	*YAR-ess-ts'ite*
secretary	(der) Sekretär/-e	*sek-reh-TAIR*
	(die) Sekre-tärin/-nen	*sek-reh-TAIR-in*
(to) see	sehen	*ZAY'en*
seen	gesehen	*gheh-ZAY'en*
seldom	selten	*ZEL-ten*
(to) sell	verkaufen	*fair-KOW-fen*
(to) send	schicken	*SHIK'en*
(to) send for	holen lassen	*HO-len LAHSS'en*
separate	verschieden, -er, -e, -es	*fair-SHEE-den*
September	(der) September	*sep-TEM-ber*

serious	ernst, -er, -e, -es	*airnst*
service	(der) Dienst/-e	*deenst*
service (hotel, restaurant)	(die) Bedien-ung/-en	*beh-DEEN-oong*
seven	sieben	*ZEE-ben*
seventeen	siebzehn	*ZEEP-ts'ayn*
seventy	siebzig	*ZEEP-ts'ikh*
several	mehrere	*MAIR-er-eh*
shares (stock)	(die) Aktien	*AHK-ts'ee-en*
shark	(der) Hai-fisch/-e	*HI-fish*
sharp	scharf, -er, -e, -es	*sharf*
she	sie	*zee*
ship	(das) Schiff/-e	*shif*
shirt	(das) Hemd/-en	*hemt*
shoe	(der) Schuh/-e	*shoo*
shop	(der) Laden/Läden	*LA-den*
short	kurz, -er, -e, -es	*koorts*
should (ought to)		
I (he, she, it) should	ich (er, sie, es) sollte	*ikh (air, zee, ess) ZOHL-teh*
you (we, they) should	Sie (wir, sie) sollten	*zee (veer, zee) ZOHL-ten*

shoulder	(die) Schulter/-n	*SHOOL-ter*
show	(die) Schau	*sh'ow*
(to) show	zeigen	*TS'I-ghen*
Show me!	Zeigen Sie mir!	*TS'I-ghen zee meer!*
shower	(das) Brausebad/-bäder	*BROW-zeh-baht*
(to) shut	schliessen	*SHLEE-sen*
sick	krank, -er, -e, -es	*krahnk*
(to) sign	unterschreiben	*oont-er-SHRY-ben*
simple	einfach, -er, -e, -es	*INE-fakh*
sincere	aufrichtig, -er, -e, -es	*OWF-rikh-tikh*
(to) sing	singen	*ZING'en*
singer	(der) Sänger/–	*ZENG-er*
sir	mein Herr	*mine hair*
sister	(die) Schwester/-n	*SHVESS-ter*
sister-in-law	(die) Schwägerin/-nen	*SHVAIG-er-in*
(to) sit	sitzen	*ZITZ'en*
Sit down!	Setzen Sie sich!	*ZETZ'en zee zikh!*
six	sechs	*zex*
sixteen	sechzehn	*ZEKH-ts'ayn*
sixty	sechzig	*ZEKH-ts'ikh*
size	(die) Größe/-n	*GRER-seh*

skin	(die) Haut/ Häute	*howt*
skirt	(der) Rock/ Röcke	*rohk*
sky	(der) Himmel	*HIM-el*
(to) sleep	schlafen	*SHLA-fen*
slow	langsam, -er, -e, -es	*LAHNG-zahm*
small	klein, -er, -e, -es	*kline*
(to) smoke	rauchen	*ROW-khen*
snow	(der) Schnee	*shnay*
so	so	*zo*
soap	(die) Seife/-n	*ZY-feh*
soft	weich, -er, -e, -es	*vy'kh*
soldier	(der) Soldat/-en	*zol-DAHT*
some (a little)	etwas	*ET-vahss*
some (several)	einige	*INE-ig-eh*
somebody	jemand	*YEH-mahnt*
something	etwas	*ET-vahss*
sometimes	manchmal	*MAHNKH-mahl*
somewhere	irgendwo	*EER-ghent-vo*
son	(der) Sohn/ Söhne	*zohn*
song	(das) Lied/-er	*leet*
soon	bald	*bahlt*
(I am) sorry.	Es tut mir leid.	*ess toot meer lite.*
soup	(die) Suppe/-n	*ZOOP-eh*

south	(der) Süden	*ZŮD-en*
South America	Süd-Amerika	*ZŮD-ah-mair-ik-ah*
South American	südamerika- nisch, -er, -e, -es	*zŮd-ah-mair- ik-AH-nish*
South American (person)	(der) Südamerikaner (die) Südamerika- nerin	*ZŮD-ah-mair- ik-ahn-er* *ZŮD-ah-mair- ik-ahn-er-in*
Spain	(das) Spanien	*SHPAHN-yen*
Spaniard	(der) Spanier/– (die Spa- nierin/-nen	*SHPAHN-ee-yer* *SHPAHN-ee-yer-in*
Spanish	spanisch, -er, -e, -es	*SHPAHN-ish*
(to) speak	sprechen	*SHPREKH'en*
special	besonder, -er, -e, es	*beh-ZOHN-der*
(to) spend (money)	*aus*geben (SP)	*OWSS-gay-ben*
(to) spend (time)	verbringen	*fair-BRING'en*
spoon	(der) Löffel/–	*LERF-el*
sport	(der) Sport/-s	*shport*
spring	(der) Frühling/-e	*FRŮ-ling*
stamp (postage)	(die) Brief- marke/-n	*BREEF-mark-eh*
star	(der) Stern/-e	*shtairn*
(to) start	*an*fangen (SP)	*AHN-fahng'en*

station (railroad)	(der) bahn-hof/-höfe	*BAHN-hohf*
(to) stay	bleiben	*BLY-ben*
steel	(der) Stahl	*shtahl*
still (quiet, not moving)	ruhig, -er, -e, -es	*ROO-ikh*
still (time)	noch immer	*nokh IM-er*
stockmarket	(die) Börse/-n	*BER-zeh*
stone	(der) Stein/-e	*shtine*
Stop!	Halt!	*hahlt!*
(to) stop (something)	*auf*hören (SP)	*OWF-her'en*
store	(der) Laden/ Läden	*LA-den*
storm	(der) Sturm/ Stürme	*shtoorm*
story	(die) Geschichte/ -n	*gheh-SHIKH-teh*
strange (odd)	sonderbar, -er, -e, -es	*ZOHN-der-bar*
street	(die) Straße/-n	*SHTRAHSS-eh*
strong	stark, -er, -e, -es	*shtark*
student	(der) Stu-dent/-en	*shtoo-DENT*
(to) study	studieren	*shtoo-DEER'en*
subway	(die) Unter-grund-bahn/-en	*OONT-er-groont-bahn*

sudden	plötzlich, -er, -e, -es	*PLERTZ-likh*
sugar	(der) Zucker	*TS'OOK-er*
suit (clothes)	(der) Anzug/An- züge	*AHN-ts'ook*
suitcase	(der) Hand- koffer	*HAHNT-koff-er*
summer	(der) Sommer/–	*ZOHM-er*
sun	(die) Sonne	*ZO-neh*
Sunday	(der) Sonntag/-e	*ZOHN-tahk*
sure	sicher, -er, -e, -es	*ZIKH-er*
surprise	(die) Über- raschung/-en	*ŭ-ber-RAHSH-oong*
sweet	süß, -er, -e, -es	*zŭss*
(to) swim	schwimmen	*SHVIM'en*
swimming pool	(das) Schwimm- bassin/-s	*SHVIM-ba-sin*
Swiss	schweizerisch, -er, -e, es	*SHVY-ts'er-ish*
Swiss (person)	(der) Schwei- zer/–	*SHVY-ts'er*
	(die) Schwei- zerin/-nen	*SHVY-ts'-er-in*
Switzerland	(die) Schweiz	*shvy'ts*

T

table	(der) Tisch/-e	*tish*
tailor	(der) Schneider/–	*SHNY-der*
(to) take	nehmen	*NAYM'en*
(to) talk a walk	spazieren gehen	*shpa-TS'EER'en GAY'en*
(to) talk	reden	*RAYD'en*
tall	groß, -er, -e, -es	*grohss*
tape	(das) Band/Bänder	*bahnt*
tape recorder	(das) Tonbandgerät	*TOHN-bahnt-gheh-rait*
tax	(die) Steuer/-n	*SHTOY-er*
taxi	(das) Taxi/-s	*TAHK-see*
tea	(der) Tee	*tay*
(to) teach	lehren	*LAIR'en*
teacher	(der) Lehrer/– (die) Lehrerin/-nen	*LAIR-er LAIR-er-in*
team	(die) Mannschaft/-en	*MAHN-shahft*
telegram	(das) Telegramm	*teh-leh-GRAHM*
telephone	(das) Telephon/-e	*teh-leh-FOHN*
television	(das) Fernsehen	*FAIRN-zay'en*

(to) tell	erzählen	*air-TS'AIL'en*
Tell him (her) . . .	Erzähle ihm (ihr) . . .	*air-TS'AIL-eh eem (eer) . . .*
temperature	(die) Temperatur/-en	*tem-per-ah-TOOR*
ten	zehn	*ts'ayn*
terrible	furchtbar, -er, -e, -es	*FOORKHT-bar*
than	als	*ahls*
(to) thank	danken	*DAHNK'en*
Thank you!	Danke!	*DAHN-keh!*
that (one)	das	*dahss*
that	daß	*dahss*
the	der (m), die (f), das (n); die (pl)	*dair, dee, dahss, dee*
theater	(das) Theater/–	*teh-AH-ter*
their	ihr (m), ihre (f), ihr (n); ihre (pl)	*eer, eer-eh eer, eer-eh*
them	sie	*zee*
(to) them	ihnen	*EEN-en*
then	dann	*dahn*
there	dort	*dort*
there is, there are	es gibt	*ess ghipt*
therefore	deswegen	*DESS-vayg-en*
these	diese	*DEE-zeh*

they	sie	*zee*
thin	dünn, -er, -es, -e	*dün*
thing	(die) Sache/-n	*ZA-kheh*
(to) think	denken	*DEHNK'en*
third	dritt, -er, -e, -es	*drit*
thirsty	durstig, -er, -e, -es	*DOOR-shtikh*
thirteen	dreizehn	*DRY-ts'ayn*
thirty	dreißig	*DRY-sikh*
this	dies, -er, -e, -es	*dees*
those	jene	*YEH-neh*
thousand	(das) Tausend/-e	*T'OW-zent*
thread	(der) Faden/ Fäden	*FA-den*
three	drei	*dry*
throat	(die) Gurgel/-n	*GOOR-ghel*
through	durch	*doorkh*
Thursday	(der) Donners-tag/-e	*DOHN-ers-tahk*
ticket (train)	(die) Fahr-karte/-n	*FAR-kar-teh*
tie	(die) Krawatte/-n	*kar-VA-teh*
tiger	(der) Tiger/–	*TEE-gher*
time	(die) Zeit/-en	*ts'ite*
tip	(das) Trink-geld/-er	*TRINK-ghelt*
tire (auto)	(der) Reifen/–	*RY-fen*

tired	müde, müder, müde, müdes	*MÜD-eh*
to (direction)	nach	*nahkh*
to (in order to)	um . . . zu	*oom . . . ts'oo*
to the (indirect object)	dem (m, n) der (f) den (pl)	*dem* *dair* *den*
to the (place)	zu dem *or* zum (m, n) zu der *or* zur (f) zu den (pl)	*ts'oo dem, ts'oom* *ts'oo dair, ts'oor* *ts'oo den*
tobacco	(der) Tabak	*TA-bahk*
today	heute	*HOY-teh*
together	zusammen	*ts'oo-ZA-men*
tomorrow	morgen	*MOHR-ghen*
tomorrow morning	morgen früh	*MOHR-ghen frü*
tomorrow night	morgen abend	*MOHR-ghen AH-bent*
tongue	(die) Zunge/-n	*TS'OONG-eh*
tonight	heute abend	*HOY-teh AH-bent*
too (also)	auch	*owkh*
too (excessive)	allzu	*AHL-ts'oo*
tooth	(der) Zahn/Zähne	*ts'ahn*
toothbrush	(die) Zahn-bürste/-n	*TS'AHN-bür-steh*
toothpaste	(die) Zahnpaste	*TS'AHN-pa-steh*
tour	(die) Tour/-en	*toor*

towel	(das) Hand-tuch/-tücher	*HAHNT-tookh*
tower	(der) Turm/Türme	*toorm*
town	(die) Stadt/Städte	*shtaht*
toy	(das) Spielzeug/-e	*SHPEEL-ts'oyk*
trade fair	(die) Handels-messe/-n	*HAHN-delss-mess-eh*
traffic	(der) Verkehr	*fair-KAIR*
train	(der) Zug/Züge	*ts'ook*
translation	(die) Über-setzung/-en	*ů-ber-ZETS-oong*
(to) travel	reisen	*RY-zen*
travel agency	(das) Reisebüro/-s	*RY-zeh-bů-ro*
traveler	(der) Reisende/-n	*RY-zen-deh*
	(die) Reisende/-n	*RY-zen-deh*
treasurer	(der) Zahl-meister/–	*TS'AHL-my-ster*
tree	(der) Baum/Bäume	*b'owm*
trip	(die) Reise/-n	*RY-zeh*
trouble (care)	(die) Sorge/-n	*ZORG-eh*
truck	(der) Lastwagen/–	*LAHST-va-ghen*
true	wahr, -er, -e, -es	*var*

(to) try (attempt)	versuchen	*fair-ZOOKH'en*
(to) try (for quality)	probieren	*pro-BEER'en*
Tuesday	(der) Dienstag/-e	*DEENSS-tahk*
Turk	(der) Türke/-n (die) Türkin/ -nen	*TÜR-keh* *TÜR-kin*
Turkey	(die) Türkei	*tůr-KYE*
Turkish	türkisch, -er, -e, -es	*TÜR-kish*
(to make a) turn	*ab*biegen (SP)	*AHB-beeg'n*
(to) turn off	*ab*stellen (SP)	*AHP-shtel'en*
(to) turn on	*an*stellen (SP)	*AHN-shtel'en*
twelve	zwölf	*ts'verlf*
twenty	zwanzig	*TS'VAHN-ts'ikh*
two	zwei	*ts'vye*
typewriter	(die) Schreib- maschine/-n	*SHRIPE-ma-shee-neh*

U

ugly	häßlich, -er, -e, -es	*HESS-likh*
umbrella	(der) Regen- schirm/-e	*RAY-ghen-sheerm*
uncle	(der) Onkel	*OHN-kel*
under	unter	*OON-ter*

(to) understand	verstehen	*fair-SHTAY'en*
Do you understand?	Verstehen Sie?	*fair-SHTAY'en zee?*
I don't understand.	Ich verstehe nicht.	*ikh fair-SHTAY-eh nikht.*
underwear	(die) Unterkleider (pl)	*OON-ter-kly-der*
unfortunately	leider	*LYE-der*
uniform	(die) Uniform/-en	*oon-nee-FORM*
United States	(die) Vereinigten Staaten	*fair-INE-ig-ten SHTAHT-en*
United Nations	(die) Vereinten Nationen	*fair-INE-ten nah-TS'YO-nen*
university	(die) Universität/-en	*oo-nee-vair-zee-TAYT*
until	bis	*biss*
up	hinauf	*hin-OWF*
urgent	dringend, -er, -e, -es	*DRING-ent*
us, to us	uns	*oonss*
(to) use	gebrauchen	*gheh-BROW-khen*
used to (in the habit of . . .)	angewöhnt, -er, -e, -es	*AHN-gheh-vernt*
useful	nützlich, -er, -e, -es	*NŮTS-likh*
usual	gewöhnlich, -er, -e, -es	*gheh-VERN-likh*

V

vacant	unbesetzt, -er, -e, -es	*OON-beh-zetst*
vacation	(der) Urlaub	*OOR-l'owp*
vaccination	(die) Schutz-impfung/-en	*SHOOTZ-imp-foong*
valley	(das) Tal/ Täler	*tahl*
value	wert	*vairt*
various	verschieden, -er, -e, -es	*fair-SHEED-en*
very	sehr	*zair*
very well	sehr gut	*zair goot*
view	(die) Aussicht/-en	*OWSS-sikht*
village	(das) Dorf/Dörfer	*dorf*
(to) visit	besuchen	*beh-ZOOKH'en*
violin	(die) Geige/-n	*GUY-gheh*
voice	(die) Stimme/-n	*SHTIM-eh*
voyage	(die) Reise/-n	*RY-zeh*

W

(to) wait	warten	*VAR-ten*
waiter	(der) Kellner/–	*KELL-ner*

waitress	(die) Kellner-in/-nen	*KELL-ner-in*
(to) walk	gehen	*GAY'en*
wall	(die) Wand/ Wände	*vahnt*
wallet	(die) Geld-tasche/-n	*GHELT-ta-sheh*
(to) want	wollen	*VOHL'en*
I want	ich will	*vill*
he (she) wants	er (sie) will	*vill*
you (we, they) want	Sie (wir, sie) wollen	*VOHL'en*
Do you want . . . ?	Wollen Sie . . . ?	*VOHL'en zee . . . ?*
war	(der) Krieg/-e	*kreek*
warm	warm, -er, -e, -es	*varm*
(I, he, she, it) was	(ich, er, sie, es) war	*var*
(to) wash	waschen	*VAHSH'en*
watch	(die) Uhr/-en	*oor*
(to) watch	*an*schauen (SP)	*AHN-sh'ow'en*
Watch out!	Aufpassen!	*OWF-pahss'en!*
water	(das) Wasser	*VAHSS-er*
way	(der) Weg/-e	*vehk*
we	wir	*veer*
weak	schwach, -er, -e, -es,	*shvahkh*
(to) wear	tragen	*TRA-ghen*

weather	(das) Wetter	*VET-er*
wedding	(die) Hoch-zeit/-en	*HOKH-ts'ite*
Wednesday	(der) Mitt-woch/-e	*MIT-vohkh*
week	(die) Woche/-n	*VO-kheh*
weekend	(das) Wochen-ende/-n	*VO-khen-end-eh*
Welcome!	Willkommen!	*veel-KOHM'en!*
You are welcome.	Bitte schön.	*BIT-teh shern.*
well	gut	*goot*
went		
I went	ich bin ge-gangen	*gheh-GAHNG-en*
he (she, it) went	er (sie, es) ist gegangen	*air (zee, ess) isst*
you (we, they) went	Sie (wir, sie) sind gegan-gen	*zee (veer, zee) zint*
(you, we, they) were	(sie, wir, sie) waren	*VAR'en*
west	(der) Westen	*VEST-en*
what	was	*vahss*
What's the matter?	Was ist los?	*vahss isst lohss?*
What time is it?	Wie spät ist es?	*vee shpayt isst ess?*
when?	wann?	*vahn?*
when (while)	als	*ahlss*
where?	wo?	*vo?*

Where to?	Wohin?	*vo-HIN?*
whether	ob	*ohp*
which	der, die, das	*dair, dee, dahss*
which?	welcher, welche, welches?	*VEL-kher, -kheh, -khess?*
while	während	*VAIR-ent*
white	weiß, -er, -e, -es	*vice*
who?	wer?	*vair?*
who	der, die, das	*dair, dee, dahss*
whole	ganz, -er, -e, -es	*gahnts*
whom?	wen?	*vain?*
whose?	wessen?	*VESS-en?*
why?	warum?	*va-ROOM?*
wide	breit, -er, -e, -es	*brite*
widow	(die) Witwe/-n	*VIT-veh*
widower	(der) Witwer/–	*VIT-ver*
wife	(die) Frau/-en	*fr'ow*
wild	wild, -er, -e, es	*vilt*
will		
I will	Ich werde	*ikh VAIR-deh*
he (she, it) will	er (sie, es) wird	*air (zee, ess) veert*
you (we, they) will	Sie (wir, sie) werden	*zee (veer, zee) VAIR-den*
(to) win	gewinnen	*gheh-VINN'en*
wind	(der) Wind/-e	*vint*
window	(das) Fenster/–	*FEN-ster*

wine	(der) Wein/-e	*vine*
winter	(der) Winter/–	*VIN-ter*
wish	(der) Wunsch/ Wünsche	*voonsh*
(to) wish	wünschen	*VǛN-shen*
without	ohne	*OH-ne*
with the	mit dem (m, n) mit der (f) mit den (pl)	*mit daim* *mit dair* *mit dain*
wolf	(der) Wolf/ Wölfe	*vohlf*
woman	(die) Frau/-en	*fr'ow*
wonderful	wunderbar, -er, -e, -es	*VOON-der-bar*
won't		

Use **nicht** with the forms of **werden**. (See "will.")

wood	(der) Wald/ Wälder	*vahlt*
wool	(die) Wolle	*VO-leh*
word	(das) Wort/ Wörter	*vort*
work	(die) Arbeit/-en	*AR-bite*
(to) work	arbeiten	*AR-bite'en*
world	(die) Welt/-en	*velt*
worse	schlechter, -er, -e, -es	*SHLEKHT-er*
would		
I (he, she, it) would	ich (er, sie, es) würde	*ikh (air, zee, ess)* *VǛR-deh*

you (we, they) would	Sie (wir, sie) würden	*zee (veer, zee) VÛR-den*
Would you . . . ?	Würden Sie . . . ?	*VÛR-den zee . . . ?*
I would like . . .	Ich möchte . . .	*ikh MERKH-teh . . .*
Would you like . . . ?	Möchten Sie . . . ?	*MERKH-ten zee . . . ?*
(to) write	schreiben	*SHRY-ben*
Write it!	Schreiben Sie es!	*SHRY-ben zee ess!*
writer	(der) Schrift- steller/–	*SHRIFT-shtel-er*
	(die) Schrift- stellerin/-nen	*SHRIFT-shtel-er-in*
wrong	falsch, -er, -e, -es	*fahlsh*

Y

year	(das) Jahr/-e	*yar*
yellow	gelb, -er, -e, -es	*ghelp*
yes	ja	*ya*
yesterday	gestern	*GHEH-stern*
yet	jedoch	*yeh-DOHKH*
you	Sie (polite, sing or pl)	*zee*
young	jung, -er, -e, -es	*yoong*

| your | Ihr (m), Ihre (f) Ihr (n); Ihre (pl) | *eer, EER-eh* |

Z

| zipper | (der) Reißver-
schluß/
-schlüsse | *RICE-fair-shlooss* |
| zoo | (der) Zoo/-s | *ts'o* |

POINT TO THE ANSWER

To make sure that you understand the answer to your question, show the sentence in German after the arrow to the person you are addressing so that he or she can point to a reply.

 Zeigen Sie bitte auf der nächste Seite Ihr Antwort auf meine Frage. Vielen Dank.

Ja.   **Nein.**   **Vielleicht.**   **Später.**   **Sofort.**
Yes.   No.   Perhaps.   Later.   At once.

Bestimmt.   **In Ordnung.**   **Entschuldigung.**
Certainly.   All right.   Excuse me.

Ich verstehe.   **Ich verstehe nicht.**
I understand.   I don't understand.

Was möchten Sie?   **Ich weiß.**   **Ich weiß nicht.**
What do you want?   I know.   I don't know.

Offen.   **Geschlossen.**   **Zu viel.**   **Nicht genug.**
Open.   Closed.   Too much.   Not enough.

Kein Zugang.   **Es ist verboten.**
No admittance.   It is forbidden.

Einverstanden.   **Sehr gut.**   **Es ist nicht gut.**
It is agreed.   Very good.   It isn't good.

Es ist in der Nähe.   **Zu weit.**   **Sehr weit.**
It's near.   Too far.   Very far.

Links abbiegen!   **Rechts abbiegen!**
Turn left!   Turn right!

Immer geradeaus!   **Kommen Sie mit mir!**
Go straight ahead!   Come with me!

Warten Sie auf mich.   **Ich muß gehen.**
Wait for me.   I must go.

Kommen Sie später zurück.   **Ich bin gleich wieder da.**
Come back later.   I'll be right back.

Mein Name ist _____ .   **Ihr Name?**
My name is _____ .   Your name?

Telefonnummer?   **Adresse?**
Telephone number?   Address?